Someone Knows . . .

Highlighting South Dakota's Cold Cases

Christine Mager Wevik

BURLWOOD PRESS

Copyright © by Christine Mager Wevik

Cover design by Samantha Lund-Hillmer and Daniel Wevik

Interior design by Prairie Hearth Publishing, LLC

ISBN: 9798218017705

All rights reserved. No part of this work may be reproduced or transmitted by any means, electronic or mechanical, including photocopying and recording, or by any information storage or retrieval system, except as may be expressly permitted by the author.

To all the families of lost loved ones –

May you find peace and comfort in the knowledge that their names will live on a little while longer.

Foreword

As an investigative reporter, working on a series on cold cases in South Dakota, I found Chris Wevik to be a wealth of information on dozens of cases. For years, Chris has been driven to gather clues on cases that have gone cold, lest they be forgotten. Chris provides an incredible amount of detail on many of these cases. She does this from an objective point of view, the way a journalist gathers facts. Her dedication to this work is in hopes that it may lead to a crime being solved.

Many missing and murdered indigenous people's (MMIP) cases sadly receive little attention and it is often difficult to get many details because tribal members may mistrust outsiders. Chris was able to speak to family members of many missing or murdered Native Americans in South Dakota to personalize their stories, providing the reader with new insight into their cases. You can feel the heartbreak of families who wrote letters to their missing or dead loved ones throughout the book.

Chris is spot on with her title, *Someone Knows*. Someone out there does know something about each cold case. Thanks to this project, some may be solved, bringing much-needed closure to their families. The reader will find themselves becoming amateur sleuths as they make their way through the 52 cases contained within these pages. Perhaps *you* are the someone who knows.

~ Angela Kennecke
Emmy Award-winning Journalist

Preface

If you've come here looking for sensationalism, speculation, rumors, gore, drama, or conspiracies, you've come to the wrong place.

What follows are accurate cold case accounts (as accurate as possible), through law enforcement agencies, family members, or multiple news sources, and tributes from family members and friends of those victims, if available.

All attempts were made to seek the facts, and all the information in this book is credited to the source in which I found it. Therefore, any information that is conflicting or inconsistent, whether correct, incorrect, incomplete, or biased, based on what I could find, is not my intention or responsibility. Perhaps those inconsistencies will open our minds, our conversations, and the door to eventual answers.

As for photos, I included only those offered by the families or news sources in which I had written permission to publish. Regardless, I feel compelled to offer my apologies for the lack of something I feel is so vital to each story. Most of the missing persons listed in this book can be found elsewhere on the internet, including photos provided by local law enforcement.

In the course of researching and writing this book, I've discovered over 150 cases of unsolved deaths and missing persons dating back to 1969. To go back any further might be an exercise in futility, as the perpetrators of those crimes would likely be beyond the reach of prosecution or dead.

It is simply my hope to bring light to these cases that are shut away for lack of leads and perhaps see one or more of them solved. All the victims listed in this book are deserving of so much more attention than my paltry words might garner; they deserve justice, and at the very least, to be remembered.

Writing, using my imagination to entertain, has always been my passion. Finding that there were so many unsolved cases, though, has led me to feel a sense of duty to use my ability not just for entertainment, but also for something worthwhile and lasting. I want to make a difference.

To that end, I intend to support local charities such as the South Dakota Network Against Family Violence and Sexual Assault, who advocate for victims of family violence and sexual assault, and the Red Ribbon Skirt Society, an organization founded and led by Indigenous women, which promotes awareness and education about the epidemic of Missing and Murdered Indigenous Women, Children, and Two Spirit. Please consider donating to these or a local charity of your choice.

If you or someone you know has any tips regarding any of these cases, please contact the authorities listed at the end of each case or call your local Crime Stoppers to leave an anonymous tip.

Table of Contents

Introduction	i
"A Testament to Hope and Perseverance"	iii
Richynda Roubideaux	1
Arden Anderson	7
Alejandro Vasquez	11
Jesse Wallace Cook	15
Tammy Haas	17
"Other People"	37
Neil Little Eagle	39
Clara Olson	45
Stanley Strole	49
Eugene Prins	53
East Lee	63
"Journey of Unknowns"	67
Ladonna, Brian, and Patrick Mathis	69
Robert Odman	77
Cody Ray Rodriguez	81
Beverly Ulrich	93
Carmen Charger and Delmas Traversie, Jr.	97
"Information Request"	101
Alicia Folkers Hummel	103
Morgan Bauer	111
Cody White Pipe	123
Dana Adamson	129
Stanley Harris	137
"Startling Statistics"	139
Alize Millard	141
Jon Rice	145
Donna Lass	153
Mariah High Hawk	161

Ellabeth Lodermeier	169
"The Cruelty of Closure"	175
Jean Janis	177
Rachel Cyriacks	179
Charles "Charley Boy" Quiver	185
Pamela Dunn	189
Kelly Robinson	201
Pah Pow	209
Katrina Wind	213
Morgan Lewis	217
Kevin Marshall	231
Pamela Halverson	237
Axel Christensen	241
Donna Marie Larrabee	243
Joleen Hass	245
Arnold Archambeau and Ruby Bruguier	249
Robert Ghostbear	261
Serenity Dennard	265
"Two Deaths"	271
Everett and Louella Owens	273
Andrew Lufkins	275
Lawrence Steiger and Renae Uithoven	279
Larissa Lone Hill	281
Monica Wickre	287
Delema Lou Sits Poor	291
"Information Request"	294
Charles "Mesu" Quiver	295
Bonnie Rose Jennesse	299
Michael Crawford	307
Carl Bordeaux	311
Victoria Eagleman	313
Acknowledgements	321

Introduction

Someone Knows...

It might be you.

Whether you know one of these victims, you know a suspect or alibied one, you were involved in some minor or major way, or *you, in fact, are the perpetrator*, it might be *you* who knows who's responsible for one of these unsolved deaths or disappearances.

In any given unsolved case, there are almost always two people who know the perpetrator of a crime: the perpetrator, and the victim. Even then, the victim may not know his or her attacker if the perpetrator is a stranger or his or her identity is hidden. According to Statistica.com, more than half of all violent crimes are committed by someone the victim knows. A staggering 85-90% of sexual assaults are committed by someone the victim knows.

If and when any of these cases are solved, it won't be because of me or even this book. It will be because of people who continued to search for the truth, those who refused to stop talking about their loved one's death or disappearance, and those who made a promise to that loved one to seek justice on his or her behalf. Someone who spoke up and stepped up.

This book is not an investigative project. My intention has been to share whatever facts and details I could find through online sources, pose questions in each case to initiate conversation, and share law enforcement contact information. I am merely the purveyor of information. But make no mistake: it's YOU who holds the power to solve them.

How, you ask?

~ By talking: Discuss your concerns or suspicions with your friends and family, whether at home or in public. Don't let these victims fade away into oblivion. They deserve our attention, tenacity, and our unwavering devotion to see justice for them.

~ By listening: Keep a keen ear to *any* discussion you might overhear or be a part of. Many cases are solved with a seemingly minor tip; an alibi that doesn't hold water, a piece of evidence that was missed or withheld, a witness that was never questioned by authorities. Often, it's a whispered confession in a moment of passion, or a drunken boast in a crowded bar, overheard by someone who's listening. Like you.

~ By sharing: Most importantly, *share* anything you might have heard or know of or discover with law enforcement. The tiniest tip can be the biggest difference in a floundering investigation. CrimeStoppers, whose number will be shared ad nauseam in this book, accepts anonymous tips. You can call in any tip or suspicion to CrimeStoppers and you will remain completely anonymous. Promise.

~ By developing a conscience: If you know something, SPEAK UP. If you were a part of something, SPEAK UP. If you are no longer loyal to the person you alibied or suspect of a crime, SPEAK UP. Imagine your mother/child/brother is the victim and *do the right thing*.

~ And please, say their names. If we don't talk about them, and keep them alive in our searches, words, and actions, we will have abandoned them. We will have lost them all over again. And they will remain lost. Still and forever.

A Testament to Hope and Perseverance

Pamella Jackson and Cheryl Miller

Forty-two years after Pamella Jackson and Cheryl Miller went missing in rural South Dakota, the last surviving parent, Oscar Jackson, passed away at the age of 102, never knowing what happened to his daughter and her friend.

Arguably the most painful, devastating, and frustrating nightmare a parent can endure is the loss of a child who disappears without a trace, never to be seen again.

The final torchbearer, Oscar Jackson went to his grave, no doubt, with last thoughts of unanswered prayers for his missing daughter and the heaviness of guilt for not having found her.

May 29, 1971:

It's the end of the school year, and Vermillion High School students, Pamella Jackson and Cheryl Miller, both 17, made plans to attend a year-end party in rural Union County, SD. They visited Cheryl's grandmother in the Vermillion hospital and then went on to search for the party.

At approximately 9:30 pm, they met up with friends at the Garryowen Church parking lot near Spink, SD, and asked them for directions to the party at a nearby gravel pit. Driving Cheryl's grandmother's 1960 Studebaker lark, they followed their friends, three local boys, onto a gravel road leading to the quarry. The boys, briefly confused as to where to turn, missed the driveway into the quarry. When they turned around to backtrack and make their way to the party, the Studebaker's headlights that had been behind them were nowhere in sight. They arrived at the party and, not seeing the girls there, assumed the girls had changed their minds and gone home. Those boys would be the last to see the girls alive.

Thus began a more than 42-year quest to find the missing girls.

In 2004, a local man, already imprisoned in the South Dakota Penitentiary on unrelated charges, was indicted and arrested on murder charges in the case. But weeks before the case was to go to trial, the charges were dropped after the jailhouse informant who implicated him was found to have lied, and the recorded "confession" the informant offered as evidence had been fabricated.

September 23, 2013:

Three days after Oscar Jackson's funeral, a man fishing from a bridge spanning the Brule creek in southeast South Dakota spotted what appeared to be 4 wheels and the underside of a vehicle near the surface in the narrow, slow-moving stream of murky water.

Having heard the well-known and tragic story of the missing girls from that area, he immediately contacted authorities who, after painstakingly removing the rusted and crumbling car from the water, confirmed it was indeed the 1960 Studebaker Pamella Jackson and Cheryl Miller were driving.

The girls' bodies were still inside.

Authorities concluded the girls had crashed their car into the creek the night of the party while following the boys. Bolstering law enforcement's belief that no foul play was involved in the girls' deaths, the headlight switch in the car was on, the ignition was in the on position, and the car was in high gear. By all appearances, they simply lost control of the car, flipping it into the creek, and drowned.

Oscar had never given up hope that they'd be found, and

searched for them often. However serendipitously eerie and heartbreaking it is that they were found within days of his death, his hopes were fulfilled. The girls are now home with their parents.

Baby Andrew

February 28, 1981

While test driving a Jeep on the edge of town, Lee Litz caught a glimpse of something red in the ditch bordering a corn field near Sycamore Avenue in Sioux Falls, SD. Thinking it looked out of place, he pulled over to get a closer look and found it was a red blanket, soaked in blood. Upon opening it, he discovered the tiny body of a baby boy abandoned in the bitter cold. The placenta was still attached, and the cord had not been cut. The newborn's tears were still frozen to his precious face.

An autopsy determined the baby had lived for approximately two hours before succumbing to the cold and blood loss, and had been in the ditch for about 24 hours.

Sioux Falls residents, heartbroken and horrified at the utter senselessness and cruelty, collectively mourned the loss, arranging and paying for a funeral, headstone, soft PJs for Baby Andrew Doe to wear, stuffed animals to keep him company, and a pin that said, "You are loved."

Year after year, detectives revisited Baby Andrew's case, but gaining no more tips or evidence, the case remained stalled. By 2009, advancements in DNA technology prompted them to exhume little Andrew's body and acquire DNA samples. Even then, DNA matching was limited to searches in the CODIS databank, which stores DNA samples from known criminals, and did not prove useful. Every year for 10 years, detectives ran a search for a match with no results.

Finally, a welcome break in the latest technology came in the form of genetic genealogy, which combines DNA testing to traditional genealogy. Through ancestry databases, individuals seeking to discover their family lineage submit their DNA for testing, agreeing to public availability of the results. Investigators submitted Baby Andrew's DNA to an ancestry DNA testing company that found a familial connection to his mother.

They traced the family tree down to a woman in that family who would have been the appropriate and approximate age of their suspect in 1981, obtained her DNA from discarded trash, and tested it. It was a direct link to Baby Andrew's.

On what would have been Baby Andrew's 38th birthday, police showed up on the doorstep of 57-year-old Theresa Bentaas and arrested her for murder.

These two previous cold cases—now solved, decades later—are what inspired me to write this book. They stand as a testament to the hope and perseverance that we cling to in our desperate search for answers.

(Ref: *Argus Leader*; Sioux Falls; *KELO News*; Sioux Falls; *Washington Post*; Washington DC.)

Richynda Roubideaux
Unsolved Death

Richynda, affectionately known as "Richy," was born on March 16, 1986, to Elizabeth Roubideaux, on the Rosebud Sioux Reservation, Mission, SD. The third oldest of seven children, she shared her childhood with siblings Quenna (Becca), Christopher, Natalie, Brittany, Heidi, and Alvin.

Her mother describes her as bright, gentle, and happy. Passionate about the homeless, she often begged her mother to make soup or sandwiches to hand out to them, and when it was cold, found blankets to offer.

Richy excelled in school and envisioned a future life in the Air Force; perhaps someday achieving her dream of flying. Her mother has no doubt Richy would have accomplished those goals, had they not been stolen from her.

Friday, September 26, 1997, school dismissed early for the homecoming parade. 11-year-old Richy met up with her mother at the parade and asked to spend the night with her cousins. Elizabeth had never allowed her children to stay overnight away from home before but consented this time with a stern order. "Be home by noon." Richy agreed.

When Richy did not arrive at home the next day by noon, uncharacteristic for her, Elizabeth became concerned. Elizabeth then sent her oldest daughter, Becca, out to look for Richy, but she was nowhere to be found. Elizabeth then searched for her daughter. She walked to the cousins' house, where the family calmly stated, "We don't know where they are."

Elizabeth reported her missing, and initially, the local

authorities were not alarmed. They did a cursory search, but found nothing. After a few days, having no organized search, Elizabeth spoke with William Kindle, Tribal President, and John Miller, Criminal Investigator, who made posters and organized a formal search for the missing girl.

The first day of the search, October 7, 1997, Elizabeth got a tip that Richy was in Winner and opted to follow that lead rather than join the search. She was on her way to Winner when her sister met up with her and said, "Sissy, they found Richy."

Her heart not allowing her to believe the worst, Elizabeth smiled and said, "Oh, good! She must be hungry. I guess we won't need these posters anymore!"

"Sister, she's dead."

Elizabeth cried, "No! No, no, no! Show me! Take me there!" But they wouldn't allow her to see her little girl.

Richy was found outside Mission near the city sewage treatment plant, far from the road in a field, under pine trees and scrub brush. She was wearing only a t-shirt and was badly decomposed. Authorities surmised that she had been dead at least a week.

As this is an ongoing case, the autopsy report listing the cause of death has not been released. To this day, Elizabeth does not know how her little girl died or what she'd endured in her last moments.

For your consideration:

~ Who can account for the last to see little Richy? Was it the cousins or someone else who saw her last?

~ Was Richy abducted on her way home, or did she leave earlier with others?

~ Was DNA obtained from Richy's body, or is this a future possibility?

If you know any details about this crime, please contact:

1-888-577-6747 or the FBI at (605) 773-7420

Or contact the Todd County Sheriff at (605) 856-4411

Or you can call anonymously to Winner CrimeStoppers at (605) 842-3939. Phone calls are not recorded, they do not have caller ID, and you are not required to identify yourself.

(Ref: *KOTA TV; Rapid City Journal; Lakota Times*; Elizabeth Roubideaux)

My Richy – I miss you every day and night. When you was taken from me, a whole part of me died and went with you. As I grieved for you, a part of me wanted to be with you, but I prayed all the time to you to help me and give me strength to continue living for your sisters and brothers. They miss you very much, especially your oldest siblings, Becca and Chris. You three were very close. I miss when you used to come home from school and come and lay on my back, and tell me your day and tell me, "I love you, Mom. Don't worry. Be happy."

You was taken from me too soon. I wish I can go back in time and hold you a little longer. I still grieve, cry, pray to you every day and night.

I want the people, world, to know that my Richy was a bright, happy little girl. She was loved by her family and cousins and friends. Richy had a very nice personality. She loved telling jokes, crazy pranks, loved being with her friends, dancing to music. She wasn't shy. My Richy loved school. She had a future. She wanted to graduate school, and go to college and join Air Force. She wanted to fly. I believe in my heart she would've accomplished her dreams.

I miss you so much, my Richy. You have a lot of nieces and nephews and one great niece. My Richy, continue watching over your sisters, brothers, nieces, nephews, great niece. I believe my Richy is mine and our guardian angel. She's the eagle above us.

To me, it feels like it was just yesterday you was taken from me, my Richy. I pray for justice for you every day/night for you. I never got over losing you. I will forever be broken, but will remain strong for your siblings, nieces, nephews, great niece. When you come to me in my dreams and I wake up, and it's only a dream, I get very sad and pray sometimes. I catch myself thinking you're going to come home. That you're still out there somewhere, cause I never got to see you. My Richy, I love and miss you.

~ Signed, Mom. (Elizabeth Roubideaux)

*Photo courtesy of Elizabeth Roubideaux

Arden Anderson
Unsolved Death

In Langford High School's *Hoot Owl*, Langford, SD, Class of 1938, Senior Arden Anderson listed his hobby as "Hunting Gophers." His motto: "Penny earned is a penny saved," and his ambition, "Become a criminal lawyer." The Class Prophecy, enabled by the fictional invention of a machine that could see into the future, predicted "Arden Anderson, world famous criminal lawyer, up for trial for numerous shady deals with his pals, now in Alcatraz. It looks as if he will be there himself unless a miracle happens."

Arden John Fredrick Anderson was born July 11, 1921, to John C and Jennie Anderson of Langford, SD. He lived his entire life in the Langford community, graduated from Langford High School, and was engaged in farming throughout his adulthood despite his dream of becoming a criminal lawyer.

Having never married, Arden lived alone after the death of his mother. He was a member of Highlanda Lutheran Church in Langford. He often ate his evening meals alone in town, alternating between the Langford, Britton, and Webster cafes.

On the evening of Tuesday, June 21, 1983, 61-year-old Arden was found shot to death at a roadside park on Highway 12 west of Webster. According to then-Sheriff Sy Herrick in the *Langford Bugle Newspaper*, dated June 29, 1983, Mr. Anderson was attacked coming out of the men's room at the park and beaten over the head with a blunt object. Arden apparently struggled to get to his car but was shot with a .380 pistol right outside of his vehicle. He'd been seen at a Webster gas station around 9:30 p.m., and his body was discovered by a Webster area farmer at 10:05 p.m. Robbery appeared to be the motive, as Arden's wallet was not found on his body, according to then-Day County States Attorney Lonnie Vander Linden.

The news of Arden's death shook the community of Langford, and rumors circulated that perhaps someone who knew him, knew his habits, committed the murder. Those rumors still abound. It's also possible a passerby on the highway murdered him.

Arden lived a solitary, peaceful life, and was survived by several cousins and a community of lifelong friends.

For your consideration:

~ How much traffic did Highway 12 west of Webster get on the average Tuesday evening between 9:30 and 10 p.m. in 1986?

~ Who might have known that a single man, well-known

in those communities he frequented, and possibly with cash on hand, might be at that roadside park at approximately that time? Maybe someone who'd seen him earlier in the evening?

~ Who were the last to see him and interact with him? What might they know?

If you know anything about the murder of Arden Anderson, please contact:

Day County Sheriff's office at (605) 345-3222

Or leave an anonymous tip with CrimeStoppers of Aberdeen at (605) 626-3500

Thank you to Nicole Hoines, Langford Public Library, for Arden's high school information, and to Amanda Greenmyer at the *Marshall County Journal* for the newspaper clipping.

Photo courtesy of Langford Public Library

(Ref: *KELOLAND News; Langford Public Library; Marshall County Journal*)

Alejandro Pilar Vasquez
Aka "Alex" or "Tank"
Missing Person

This is Alex "Tank" Gay, also known as Alejandro Vasquez. He was born to Mario Vasquez and Josie Gay on May 6, 1991. He was the youngest of 4, joining 3 brothers, Justin, Mario, Jr., and Angel.

He grew up primarily in Kyle, SD, attending school there, and alternating time with his father, Mario, in KS.

On the weekend prior to Halloween, 2015, 24-year-old Alex arrived in South Dakota from Dodge City, KS. He was staying with his brother, Angel, in American Horse Creek, a small community about seven miles southwest of Kyle. Alex and Angel's aunt and grandmother lived within a quarter mile of Angel's, as well.

On October 29, Alex was at his brother's trailer, and

Angel heard him get up and go outside and come back in multiple times. About 3 a.m., Alex went outside without telling Angel where he was going and never returned.

Throughout the coming days and weeks, authorities conducted multiple searches with ATVs, cadaver dogs, and search aircraft. Family and friends also organized private search parties. Despite those efforts, no trace of Alex has been found.

When last seen, Alex was wearing a dark (black or gray) shirt, black or dark plaid shorts with blue stripes, and white Converse or Nike sneakers with a black stripe. He did not own a cell phone or debit or credit card at the time of his disappearance.

Earning his beloved nickname, Tank was 5'7" and 200 pounds with shoulder-length dark brown hair and brown eyes. He is of Lakota and Mexican descent and is also known to use the last name Gay, his mother's maiden name.

For your consideration:

~ With both an aunt and grandmother within a quarter mile of Angel's home, why would Alex wander off and not stop at one of these places?

~ Was Alex meeting someone? What are the odds that someone was driving around the area at 3 a.m. on a Thursday night and happened to pick him up or hurt him?

~ What motive would anyone have to pick Alex up and hurt him? Had he simply wandered off and passed out in a ditch somewhere? Why has he not been found?

If you have any information about Alex's case, please contact the Pine Ridge Police Department at (605) 867-2931

Or contact Kyle, SD Police at (605) 455-2311

Or CrimeStoppers USA at 1-800-222-8477 (or 1-800-222-TIPS)
Photo courtesy of Mario Vasquez
(Ref: *Rapid City Journal*; The Charley Project; Mario Vasquez)

"He was like a big kid to me. He had the heart of a kid. Yes, he was built like a tank, but had a big, gentle heart. Kids loved him—he was so good with them and they were his world. He was like them. He loved everyone; his nieces, his auntie, mother, grandma, me... He was loved by his family and friends.

When he was little, he'd follow me everywhere, and we'd go fishing. We'd sit there all day and fish, just him and me, and it was like there was no one else in the world but us. All alone. More like friends than father and son, in my heart and my mind, because he was so special to me.

We'd go hunting for wild turnip, you know, timpsila. We'd find them on the hills, dig them out, make bread with it, or cook them and eat them or use them in soup. Or we'd go to American Horse Creek, down by the creek, and pick cherries or plums from the wild fruit trees.

He was close with his brothers, they were always together, and his best friends were his cousins in Kyle. After his mom died, he came to live in Kansas, but after a while, it seemed he was restless. He went back and forth between Kansas and Kyle. He went back and forth, couldn't get settled.

He could draw. When he was in school in Kyle, he drew a bear one time and it was crazy—I see the drawing like it was moving. It was so real. I don't have the picture anymore. No, that's all gone. And now he's gone."

Mario Vasquez, father

Jesse Wallace Cook
Unsolved Death

Jesse Wallace Cook, a young, loving father at age 32, was found near the water tower on the corner of Willow Street and Highway 212 in Eagle Butte, unresponsive. He died shortly after he was found.

Jesse, also known as Wanblí Gleŝká/Spotted Eagle, died from blunt force trauma injury to his head with severe facial injuries.

According to an article in *West River Eagle*, Cook's father, M. Jay Cook, stated his son often hung out with friends at the water tower and had been there the night before he died, and that there had recently been a rash of violence events including harassment, theft, and beatings.

An article in the *Argus Leader* stated that Jesse was an enrolled member of Cheyenne River Sioux Tribe, and had worked several jobs in the area, including DJ at Sobriety Dances, firefighter, monitor at a local homeless shelter, and security guard for local powwows.

When Jesse died, he left behind a 10-year-old daughter, Precious, who is now living with Jesse's father.

The FBI is offering a reward of up to $10,000 for information about the murder of Jesse Wallace Cook.

If you know anything about the death of Jesse Wallace Cook, please contact
FBI's Minneapolis Field Office at (763) 569-8000
Or report anonymously to tips.fbi.gov.
(Ref: *Argus Leader; West River Eagle*)

Jesse Wallace Cook

Jesse loved his daughter, Precious. He took his daughter for strolls around town, and did everything he could to keep her comfortable and happy. He loved to go to powwows with his daughter. He helped her get started in jingle dance then, now traditional. He and his brother, Bear, started dancing when they were young.

Jesse loved to work, and helped when he could. He loved his nieces and nephews and every year during Cheyenne River Fair and Rodeo, he'd take all the kids, put them in the back of his truck, and off they'd go. We'd only see them at night. He loved them so.

We, his family, miss him so much.
Denise Fast Horse, mother

*Photo courtesy of Denise Fast Horse

Tammy Haas
Unsolved Death

"A Kind of Hush"

I began working on this book about four years ago, and Tammy's story was one of the first I researched. I got to know her wonderful mother, and found we shared many mutual friends and common connections. When I spoke with people in Yankton, it seemed I could share any salacious tidbit without a sideways glance, but the moment I spoke of Tammy's murder, voices dropped to a whisper, eyes darted, people leaned in. It brought to mind the song, "There's a Kind of Hush," made famous in the 60s by the Herman's Hermits. While the lyrics don't apply, the title resonated with me, chilled me. Someone knows. No one is talking.

What is it about this town, this precious girl that elicits such a sense of secrecy? Is it power? Loyalty? Fear? The pall that descended at the mere mention of her name unsettled me and plagued my mind with questions not only of her death, but the immediate and unnerving effect her name had on this town's residents. What is the propensity towards silence rather than thundering outcry for the justice she deserves?

This eerie and pervasive phenomenon is not unique to Yankton. I've since experienced it in many South Dakota towns in which I mention an unsolved death of their own.

Incidentally, in more than one online article and social media comment, I've seen Tammy described as "one of Yankton's own." Were I Tammy, I would know by whom I was embraced as such and by whom I was horrifically betrayed.

My own reaction to those words was unexpected, not at all a feeling of loving inclusion, imagining how Tammy might and his friend at the car wash with all the doors and trunk open, cleaning out his car after the parade.

One witness, Valerie Hoepner, claimed she saw Tammy at the homecoming parade around 4 p.m. and called out to her, but the person didn't answer, turned and went into the crowd. It seemed to be a case of mistaken identity because no one else claimed to have seen Tammy at the parade.

That evening at 5:30 p.m., Eric and Tammy were set to have a dinner date at the Black Steer Steakhouse to celebrate his upcoming birthday. The restaurant did not require reservations, so there was no way to verify this date with them, but Tammy had written a letter to a friend postmarked Sept. 17th stating they had a date there. Eric later stated that he tried calling Tammy at her aunt's house, but there was no answer. Tammy didn't show, and at 6:30 p.m., he was at his home to celebrate with his friends.

Multiple parties took place that Friday evening, and at one of them, several witnesses stated they heard the story of a young man, Jamie Horacek, urinating through Eric's open car window the night before at the Stephenson farm, and how Eric was seen cleaning out his car that day at the car wash.

~ Saturday, September 19th, 1992:

Vicki Larsen, Tammy's aunt, called a friend of Tammy's to get Eric's phone number. She hadn't seen Tammy since Thursday night, and asked Eric when he last saw her. He told her Tammy left his house on foot after midnight Thursday night/Friday morning. Eric called Tammy's friend, Dee Dee Budig, and told her that Tammy hadn't been to work.

Dee Dee started calling around, asking people if they'd

seen Tammy, and searched for Tammy around Yankton, the lake, and into Nebraska.

By 7:30 that evening, Tammy's family had filed a missing persons report with the Yankton Police Dept.

When questioned by authorities later, Eric stated that he drove around alone looking for Tammy near the airport, north of Yankton where they had attended the first party. His friend, Jason, told authorities that he and Eric drove around Gavins Point and the lake Saturday afternoon searching for Tammy.

Searches continued for Tammy around Yankton and surrounding areas throughout the weekend.

~ Monday, September 21st, 1992:

Yankton Police Department interviewed Eric about Tammy about 4 p.m.

~ Wednesday, September 23rd, 1992:

Early in the morning, between 7:30 and 8:00 a.m., Rick Kuchta, a golfer looking for errant balls, discovered a body in the ditch south of the Crofton Lakeview Golf Course in Nebraska. He contacted Nebraska authorities and the body was later identified as Tammy Haas.

Tammy's body was sent to Sioux Falls that afternoon and autopsied by pathologist Dr. Brad Randall.

That evening, Eric and two friends left to spend the night at a family cabin near Gregory, SD.

~ Thursday, September 24th, 1992: (Eric's birthday)

A second autopsy was performed on Tammy's body in Sioux City, IA, by Iowa Medical Examiner, Dr. Thomas Bennett. It was then determined that Tammy died of a neck injury called overflexion (AKA: hyperflexion, or hyperflexation). He stated this is "when the neck is injured when tilted forward, usually far enough ahead so that the chin hits the chest." He also said, "this usually is the result of a blow to the back of the head, like a fall." The injuries indicated blunt force pressure to the back of the head, damaging the upper cervical spine. She'd also a contusion on the back of her head near the base of the skull, and a severe blow to the abdomen, tearing the tissue connecting the lower intestine to the back of the abdominal wall. This injury would have knocked the wind out of her, temporarily incapacitating her. According to the medical examiner at trial, this could be attributed to a blow, a kick, or a fist, but he couldn't determine exact causation. Her cause of death is listed as hyperflexation of the neck (resulting in death), and manner of death as homicide.

Also on this date, FBI agent and a Nebraska State Patrol officer interviewed Eric.

Another party takes place, seemingly to celebrate Eric's birthday.

~ Friday, September 25th, 1992:

Eric took a lie detector test, and during the line of questioning about Tammy's death, "deception is detected."

4:15 p.m., Eric's 1988 Chevy Beretta was seized and impounded.

Eric was driven to the area where Tammy was found, and he walked directly to the spot at the top of the ravine where Tammy's body had been dumped, without direction. He later claimed in court he saw trampled grass and stopped, knowing he was in the right area due to newspaper reports and what kids had told him.

More parties took place that evening.

~ Saturday, September 26th, 1992:

Sheriff Hunhoff met with Jennifer Jones to interview her about her alleged sighting of Tammy on Thursday, the 17th. More parties took place that evening.

~ Sunday, September 27th, 1992:

Funeral home visitation took place for Tammy.

~ Monday, September 28th, 1992:

Funeral services were held for Tammy at St John's Lutheran Church.

THE INVESTIGATION:

The discovery of Tammy's body sparked a firestorm of investigations through six different agencies: Yankton City Police Department, Yankton County Sheriff's Department, South Dakota Department of Criminal Investigation, the FBI, Cedar County Sheriff's Department, and the Nebraska State Patrol. With Tammy as a South Dakota resident and her body found in Nebraska, jurisdiction became a complicating factor, according to one investigator at the YPD. But those complications did not stall or derail the investigation. The investigation involved at least 27 investigators, interviewing hundreds of people.

THE EVIDENCE:

~ Medical examiners determined by the state of Tammy's stomach contents (spaghetti she'd eaten between 5:30 and 6:30 that night), that 12:30 a.m. that night was the latest she could have died. According to an online article by Vernon J. Gebert, MS, MPS, Homicide and Forensic Consultant, "under ordinary circumstances, the stomach empties its contents four to six hours after the last meal. If the stomach is entirely empty, death probably took place four to six hours after the last meal. Various ingested food materials remain within the stomach for variable periods of time, depending on the nature and size of the meal." Spaghetti was still found in Tammy's stomach at autopsy (as well as purged from her stomach after death, in the ditch), so it's highly unlikely she died after 12:30 a.m.

~ Though this has no bearing on Tammy's death or someone's involvement, there were no drugs found in her system at the time of the autopsy; only caffeine and alcohol (two tests: .08 and .084)

~ Based on liver mortis, Tammy's body would have been dumped in the ditch within approximately a half hour after her death. And based on evidence or lack thereof, she did not die there. Evidence suggested she was rolled down the embankment, as she was found facedown, her ponytail "thrown forward, rather than laying down where it ordinarily would have been," according to Sheriff Hunhoff.

~ Tammy's time of death would almost certainly exclude the chance that Tammy had returned to Yankton and was alive and well at the time that Eric and his sister, Sarah, claimed to have seen her. The small window of opportunity for anyone else to have abducted, assaulted, and killed Tammy by 12:30 a.m., though not entirely impossible, was unrealistic, especially if Eric and Sarah were mistaken in their timeline. And the odds that Tammy was seen at Pump N Stuff, over a mile away, about the same time, would make at least one of these possibilities untrue.

~ According to an article in the *Yankton Press and Dakotan*, "Scientific evidence proves 19-year-old Tammy Haas was in the trunk of a vehicle before her body was later discovered in a ditch, an investigator said. 'As a result of scientific examinations, the task force is able to state that Tamara Haas was in the trunk of a vehicle prior to her body being found,' said Charles Draper, special agent for the FBI." And "Information last week proved Haas did not die in the ditch where she was found."

~ Hairs consistent with Tammy's were found in Eric's trunk, but based on the fact that she had used his car a number of times before her death, this was not introduced at the trial. A red, plastic fragment was found on Tammy's clothing, and three to four red, plastic fragments were also found in Eric's trunk that, with microscopy and spectrographic pyrolysis, were found to be chemically similar, though the origin of the material was never determined. Fibers that matched those in Eric's trunk were found on Tammy's clothing. Dr Reena Roy and Michael Auten, both with Nebraska State Patrol Crime Lab, stated that these could only have gotten onto her clothing through direct transfer, that someone had placed Tammy's body in Eric's trunk. Fibers found on Tammy's clothing were consistent with those on Eric's trunk mat, but could not be tied exclusively to Eric's trunk mat.

~ A vaginal swab during autopsy revealed semen present in her body. Eric had stated during interviews and trial testimony, that he and Tammy had sex on both Wednesday and Thursday (the night she disappeared). Though urine was found on the back of her underwear and on her pants (one of Eric's blood type, and one undetermined, possibly from the urine in Eric's car on the passenger seat or Tammy's own), no semen was found on her underwear. As Dr. Reena Roy from the Nebraska Criminalistics Lab testified, had Eric and Tammy "had vaginal intercourse without a condom and Tammy walked as per Eric's alibi, she would expect to find semen on the underwear 100% of the time." In other words, if Tammy had walked home, walked anywhere in fact, directly after having sex, with gravity and the amount of time she would have been upright, there is zero chance there would be no semen in her underwear.

~ No witnesses claimed to have seen Tammy walking home from Eric's the night she went missing. Law enforcement canvased the area between Eric's house and her aunt's house, and despite the numerous parties going on along that route, no one saw her. And Tammy, being well-known and friends with many of these people, might have stopped or at least been seen by someone.

~ According to Eric, Wednesday and Thursday were alike in that he and Tammy had spent time at his house, had sex, and she had walked home.

~ When Tammy's body was found, her pants had been pulled down, and hanging loose from one foot, suggesting a sexual assault had taken place. The autopsy, however, determined that no forcible sexual assault had taken place. Though semen was found, likely Eric's since he testified they'd had intercourse, there was no evidence of rape or sexual assault. Scrapes on her left calf and right buttock were suggestive that her pants were down at the time of injury. It's also possible that her pants were pulled down as she was dragged across the road to the ravine, and under the guardrail to the top of the ravine. Several small, yellow paint flecks that had reflective beads were found on her pants, consistent with yellow road paint used for striping. Officials could not determine if it specifically came from the road near where she was found.

~ Luminol, a substance that detects bodily fluids was used on Eric's car and reveals traces of bodily fluids on the dash, seat, steering wheel, and the rear of Eric's car. This could very likely have been traces of urine from the prank at the party.

~ Eric, when questioned by authorities about the prank, denied it happened, and claimed he had closed up his car and locked it at the party. Multiple witnesses heard Horacek and others laughing about the prank the night before, and Eric was seen the next day at the car wash, which he also initially denied. Later, during testimony, he denied opening the trunk.

~ Friday, September 15th, 1995:
Three days before the statute of limitations on manslaughter was to run out, Eric Stukel was arrested and charged with manslaughter. The $5000 bond was posted and he was released.

~ Wednesday, September 25th, 1996:
Trial began for Eric Stukel, charged with manslaughter.

~ Saturday, October 5th, 1996:

While the jury was in deliberation, they asked if Tammy's death had to occur in Cedar County, NE in order for Eric to be found guilty, and their answer was yes, her death by manslaughter had to occur specifically in Cedar County, NE in order to find Eric guilty. The Knox/Cedar County line is less than half a mile from where her body was found. Years later, a juror stated that the confusion was regarding which county the farmhouse was in, intimating that if the death had occurred at the Stephenson farm, in Knox County, it would have exempted Eric from being found guilty of manslaughter in *Cedar* County.

Eric Stukel was acquitted of the charge of manslaughter.

~ Multiple times throughout the years, Tammy's gravesite has been vandalized.

What follows are statements made by Eric, his friends, and Tammy's friends throughout the investigation and the trial, which, while compelling, are not proof of guilt. I'm entitling this section as . . .

HEARSAY:

~ Early Sunday morning between 3:00 and 4:00 a.m., Eric, seemingly intoxicated, entered the Fryin' Pan his parents owned and told a young man, Josh Fry, who worked there, "I think I might have killed a girl." Josh, alarmed, then told Eric's friend, Jason Adamson, as well as a manager. Jason took Eric away. Josh didn't know about Tammy at the time. He then told a girl late one night and she told him he needed to report it. He was going to report it the next day, since it was late, but she called it in on the tipline and reported this statement to the authorities. They contacted Josh Fry the next day.

~ Twice, after Tammy was reported missing, friends

asked Eric where he thought she might be. Both times, he said, "For all I know, she's probably lying dead in a ditch somewhere." When police asked Eric where she might be, he suggested that Tammy could be looking for sympathy or pity because of her unhappy home life.

~ On the Sunday after Tammy went missing, two of Tammy's friends, Marjo Swedeen and Travis Novak, visited Eric at his home. They found him in his darkened room, listening to a song he claimed was Tammy's, "Chloe Dancer." He was burning incense and candles, and he had placed photos of Tammy around them like a shrine. When they asked him about Tammy, he wouldn't respond except to talk about a book he was reading, "In the Mind's Eye." He seemed emotionally unaffected by her disappearance and didn't offer to help look for her. Another of Eric's friends claimed during testimony to have seen the "shrine" in Stukel's home.

~ Although Eric initially denied being at the car wash on Friday, after his car was impounded by the police, a friend asked if Eric was worried about what they might find. He replied, "No, they shouldn't find anything. I cleaned it out real good."

~ Throughout the weekend after the night Tammy disappeared, Eric attended many parties and hung out with friends, but according to friends and witnesses, he didn't appear to be affected by Tammy's disappearance.

For your consideration:

~ Why did Eric drive north toward the airport in his search after he learned Tammy was missing, when she left his house to walk south to her aunt's? When he told authorities he had driven north to look for her, why didn't he mention that he and a friend, Jason Adamson, drove south to look around Gavins Point and in NE for her, as Jason Adamson stated to authorities?

~ The book, "In the Mind's Eye" was published in 1991 by the National Research Council, containing a chapter on deception detection during interview situations. Is it mere coincidence that Eric happened to be reading "In the Mind's Eye" after Tammy went missing, before she was found?

~ Why would Eric deny that someone peed in his car window at the party? What possible difference would it make to authorities?

~ Why did Eric first deny going to the car wash the day after Tammy disappeared? If he had nothing to do with her disappearance, what difference would it make to authorities if he had?

~ Once multiple witnesses stated that he was at the car wash on Friday, why would Eric deny it rather than admit he was cleaning urine from his car?

~ When Tammy stood him up for his date on Friday at the Black Steer, why didn't he drive to her aunt's house? He stated he tried calling her, but wouldn't any typical boyfriend wonder what was wrong, why his girlfriend didn't show up for a date? And why weren't authorities able to verify his phone calls to Tammy's aunt's home?

~ Why wouldn't Eric just show up at her house the night she "stood him up," instead of trying to call repeatedly? Did they make arrangements to meet there or was he to pick her up? Why would he pick her up the night before, Thursday, but not this night? In fact, he'd met Tammy's aunt, Vicki, for the first time at Vicki's house just the night before. So he apparently picked Tammy up Wednesday night as well, and knew where the house was.

~ This is not proof of anything, but how do Eric and friends continue to party after she's reported missing?

~ Is it possible that Eric, Sarah, and Jennifer Jones at Pump N Stuff had their nights mixed up, since Eric stated that Wednesday and Thursday were repeats of their actions at his home? Especially given that Jennifer stated in court that Tammy's hair was down, but in a ponytail when her body was found.

~ The proximity of the location of the party to where Tammy's body was found is less than two miles and cannot be ignored. What are the odds that Tammy made it back to Yankton to Eric's home eight or so miles away, after the party, with her time of death no later than 12:30 a.m., and her body dumped into the ravine by approximately 1 a.m.?

~ Is it possible that Eric was telling the truth about closing up his car and locking it the night of the party, but that Tammy had left the window down without his knowledge? That maybe he discovered the urine when they went to leave the party, and her negligence in rolling up her window?

~ Were fingerprints ever found on Tammy's purse or shoes? Can advancements in technology help recover possible prints?

~ Have DNA tests been done to determine whose urine and semen was found in and on Tammy's body and clothing? Will there someday be more tests done to seek new information?

~ Did the final question by the jury and the subsequent answer keep Eric from being found guilty? Or was it lack of evidence?

While I pose these questions, keep in mind that Eric

was acquitted—found not guilty—in Tammy's death. Although there are endless questions, untruths, and secrets surrounding involved parties' actions and reactions regarding her disappearance and death, there was not enough physical evidence to tie Eric to her death, and what evidence there is, is largely circumstantial. Therefore, simple logic behooves us to consider other suspects and possibilities.

If you know any details about the death of Tammy Haas, please contact:
Yankton Police Department at (605) 668-5210
FBI office in Sioux Falls at (605) 334-6881
Online at tips.fbi.gov
Or anonymously at Yankton CrimeStoppers at (605) 665-4440

The FBI Minneapolis Office and the Yankton Police Department are offering a $15,000 reward for information regarding the death of Tammy Haas.

(Ref: *Yankton Press & Dakotan, Argus Leader*, verification through court transcripts, Nancy Haas, Chad Zimmerman, Gary Idt.)

Dear Tammy (Tamara Ann),

You lost your life at the age of 19 by the hands of another who then, either on their own or help of others, threw you down a hill to lie for 5 nights and 5 days.

Your brothers were only 16 and 12 years old and had already lost theirs and your father at the age of 38, 3 years before.

I want you to know we loved you then and love you now while your home is in Heaven because of your faith.

We miss your smile and laughter. Your kindness to everyone. We know you would, as we want to also, forgive those who were involved and those who know, but were not involved with your death, to just come forward with the <u>truth</u>.

I know you would want me to thank all who have worked

hard to find answers and have given their time and funding.
You will never be forgotten!
Love you always,
Mom (Nancy Haas)

*Photo courtesy of Nancy Haas

"People are like stained-glass windows. They sparkle and shine when the sun is out, but when the darkness sets in, their true beauty is revealed only if there is a light from within." ~ Elisabeth Kubler-Ross

Tammy had a vivacious spirit and it drew people into her realm. If you met Tammy, she considered you a friend for life. She had friends from many different social circles. She didn't care about your social, economic or academic standing. Tammy cared whether or not you were a good person. Whenever I think of the saying "Don't judge a book by its cover," she comes to mind. I met many people I would have not normally let into my circle, if it hadn't been for her. In all the people I have talked to over the years, I have never heard a negative word said about her.

Tammy was the type of person who walked into a room and the energy lifted. Her laughter was contagious. It came from deep inside her and out into the world. It was a magical sound and I still hear it sometimes in my memory and I cannot help but smile.

Because there wasn't a lot to do in Yankton, we would spend countless hours driving around town and out to the lake. Her bare feet would be on the dash and we would be laughing and singing along to Pearl Jam, REM or NIN. We were two girls with no clear destination but enjoying life. I miss those carefree days!

In our years of friendship, I only remember her crying once and it was when she learned her dad had passed. The loss of her dad devastated her, but she didn't let it define her. Shortly after the funeral, I saw her walking down the hall with her mega-watt smile. I once asked her how she could carry on so easily, she said it wasn't easy but she didn't want to bring other people down.

The amazing thing about Tammy is outwardly she was absolutely stunning, but inside she had this outstanding, loving spirit, which blew away her outside appearance. When I think of Tam, the phrase "love for life" comes to mind.

When Tammy danced on stage, you were drawn to her. She brought such grace and beauty to the stage; her presence commanded attention. It was a magical experience to watch her dance so effortlessly. Her feet would glide across the stage almost as if she was floating. When she danced, she took you along her journey.

We corresponded our freshman year of college via letters and phone calls. I considered her one of my closest friends. I fondly remember our freshman year as one of those thrilling and expectant times; our whole lives ahead of us and enjoying the freedom college allows. A year later, all of that would change.

When I heard she was missing, my heart sunk. It was so unlike her to not be in touch with anyone. It was especially hard to comprehend since the night she went missing; she was supposed to be with me and our mutual friend, Trav. I clung desperately to the hope she would be found safe and sound. Her tragic death turned everything right in the world, upside down and crooked. Tragic endings are not supposed to happen in small town USA and it struck every fiber in my *being because of the injustice and offense.*

To still be waiting for answers after all these years leaves an inconceivable pain that only the truth can heal. I would love to remember Tammy as she was as opposed to how she died. She brought radiance and passion to this world and her untimely death brought darkness and pain. Tam deserved more than her ending. She deserved a full story and not the devastating result of what transpired that night and the continuing saga of mystery surrounding her unexpected death. Tammy deserves to be remembered as the wonderful, gregarious person she was and not remembered as the image of body bag being lifted out from a ravine.

Marjo (Swedeen) Rollin, friend

Other People

Anyone who's ever watched a true crime show has heard someone say, "This happens to other people, not us."

Who are the "other people?"

Answer: People. People of all colors. People of all walks of life. Us.

What if you haven't been personally affected by violent crime? How close have we come without our knowledge?

We don't know how closely we may have skirted tragedy; that narrow miss on the two-lane highway, avoiding the drunk or texter; that stranger following you that changed their plan; that locked door; that light that came on at just the right moment; the stranger helping you who happened to be good rather than evil.

There's no statistic telling us how close we've come to becoming a statistic, or telling us how fortunate we are that we aren't "other people."

Perhaps our understanding of others' "if only's" might be the eraser of the thinnest line called "chance" that separates us.

Neil "Mesu" Little Eagle
Missing Person

Neil "Mesu" Little Eagle disappeared from Porcupine, SD, on July 27th, 2017, and was never seen again.

Neil may use his nickname, "Mesu," and may ask for directions to Scottsbluff, NE.

According to Neil's older sister, Petula, the year he went missing, she'd gotten several calls from their cousins, Virginia and Debra, asking her for money because they couldn't get Neil to sign documents allowing them to get SSI and food stamps on his behalf. Petula couldn't afford a place of her own or a car, but she offered to try to scrape up enough to send her sister, Mary, who would take them money to help pay for food for Neil. She states that within days of those phone calls, and before she could get ahold of

Mary to send her money for Neil, he went missing.

Once Petula heard of Neil's disappearance, she and her sister, Mary, went to Pine Ridge and spoke with John Pettigrew, Pine Ridge investigator, who told them that Neil was found walking on a road in NE and taken to Pine Ridge.

A man posted on Facebook that he had picked up Neil on July 20th, 2017, or someone he believed was Neil, near Merriman, NE. It was hot out, and Neil was walking, had taken his shirt off, and was carrying two empty water bottles. He seemed disoriented and didn't know where he was or how he got there. The man gave him a ride to Pine Ridge, SD, and turned him over to police.

John Pettigrew states he then took Neil from Pine Ridge to Virginia's in Porcupine, and that was the last time he was seen by police officers.

Petula states that Virginia, who had Power of Attorney over Neil and with whom he was staying, claimed that she'd had to run an errand and left her grandson to watch over Neil. Virginia claims that when she returned home, her grandson told her that he'd gone into the restroom, and when he came out, Neil was at the end of the driveway, getting into a dark-colored vehicle.

Cheryl, Neil's oldest sister, states that Virginia had arranged to get Neil into a local nursing home where he could be cared for with his worsening seizures and dementia. Neil, never wanting to be in any facility or tied down to one location, may have run off to avoid moving to a nursing home.

Another missing person poster (pictured in a Facebook post about his disappearance) had been amended in handwriting, claiming Neil was spotted in Rushville, NE, on July 28th, 2017, but those claims have not been substantiated.

Neil is approximately 5'3" to 5'5" and 135-145 pounds, with black hair and dark brown eyes. He was last seen wearing a black jacket, white t-shirt, dark gray sweatpants and light gray, high-top Nike shoes. It's also reported he was wearing a red shirt and red shorts. Neil is legally blind, suffers from dementia and seizures, and did not have his necessary medication with him when he went missing.

For your consideration:
~ The timeline regarding Neil's whereabouts is confusing as to when police and family last saw him. Did Neil have a habit of disappearing, which made it hard to nail down an exact time he went missing?

~ There are various reports that he (or someone who was blind and having seizures, but they didn't know who he was) was in a hospital in Scottsbluff, NE in May of 2019, and that he was transferred to a nursing home facility in NE or CO, but they didn't know where. Wouldn't a hospital have to have positive identification of a person before transferring him to another facility, which would *also* have to have positive identification of a person before admitting? Wouldn't a hospital require meticulous records of any patients they've treated?

~ When Neil's sisters, Cheryl and Petula, question authorities about his case, they're told it's an ongoing case, but don't return calls or give them updates. Why?

If you know anything about Neil "Mesu" Little Eagle's disappearance, please contact
Pine Ridge Police at (605) 867-8127.
Photo courtesy of Petula Duarte
(Ref: The Charley Project, Petula Duarte, Cheryl Little Eagle)

Mesu is my little brother. Me and him speak our language fluently since we were very young. English was our second language. We would take our grandparents to offices and interpret what they told us to in English. Lots of people thought that was very cute.

I miss him daily—our talks, our everyday joking around.

He's a very polite man—holds doors for people, he will not sit back and watch you work; he will do it for you, while talking about how grandparents and dad told him and showed him how to help people.

Unfortunately, he almost died a few times. Our uncles used to tease him, "he's a cat and has nine lives." Me and my children and grandchildren miss him a lot, because he's always joking, giving advice, etc. . .

Since he's been missing, a big part of us is missing also.

Cheryl Little Eagle
*Photo courtesy of Cheryl Little Eagle

Neil Little Eagle (Mesu)

My little brother, it's been so long since the last time I saw you. I didn't realize it then, that it would be the last time I would see you, hear your voice, see your smile for the last time. The last time I would actually hug you and tell you I love you. I would give anything to go back to that day, and just take you with me to Colorado. I regret not taking you with me. I shed tears every day, fight this deep depression, and pray that you will be found, safe. I pray for our little sister Mary, who suffers as much as I do. We both live with this emptiness in our hearts, we would give anything to see you again, hear your voice, see your smile, hear you joking around, making us laugh.

You are such a good person, with a great sense of humor, yet so caring, always putting others above yourself. The best mechanic we know. You did so much for others, but we all let you down, when you needed us the most. I apologize for not being there to protect you from whatever happened to you. I will live the rest of my life, wondering what happened to you, living with this pain and emptiness in my heart, because my only brother is gone, without a trace.

I often question my faith, ask God, "Why my brother? Please bring him home, guide me to find him! Bring him home!" But the years pass by, nothing! Where is the justice?! We need closure!

Sometimes, on my saddest days, I'm missing you, and out of nowhere, Billy Joe Royal songs come on, and I feel you're trying to cheer me up. I remember how excited you were to introduce me to his music. I remember we would go cruising, listening to all of his songs, drive to the lake, just listening to Billy Joe Royal. Precious memories that live in my heart forever.

I will never forget you. I will not rest until I get closure. I just need to find you. I still hold onto hope, that maybe you are in a nursing home. That's what keeps me going, keeps my hopes alive. Because I have no quality of life, not knowing where my brother is.

My kids will remember your comedy moments and we share a good laugh, and we express our love for you, how much we miss you. I will not rest until I find you and get justice. I will try to be strong for you, for our little sister Mary, who suffers your absence as much as I do. We will not give up until you are located. I love you forever, my little brother.

Your big sister, Petula Little Eagle-Duarte

Clara Olson
Unsolved Death

Henry Olson, rural Renner, South Dakota, spoke with his mother, Clara Olson, every day. August 6th, 1986, however, he didn't get a call from her, and when he called her, no one answered. Henry grew concerned, as his 93-year old mother lived alone in an apartment in Sioux Falls. He immediately left for Sioux Falls to check on her.

When he arrived at the apartment, he found his mother dead in her bed and called authorities. It wasn't until a funeral director discovered faint bruising around Clara's neck that her cause of death, at first considered "natural," became a case of homicide. By then, valuable evidence had been lost, accidentally destroyed. By this time, the odds of ever solving this crime were incredibly diminished.

Clara, a tiny, frail woman, clearly not a threat to anyone,

was strangled. Police did not disclose if her residence showed signs of forced entry or a struggle, but Clara's body did show multiple injuries.

Clara and her husband, also named Henry, had lived in the house on West 11th Street 30 years after he retired from farming. He had then worked as a custodian for the Veteran's Hospital, and she'd worked as a housekeeper for then-Sioux Valley Hospital. Her husband had passed away 10 years before, and she had retired from housekeeping about 15 years before her death.

Family, neighbors, and friends described her as sweet, caring, and kind. Clara lived alone in the first-floor apartment, and managed the four-unit building, collecting rent from the other renters. Though Clara seemingly had no enemies that anyone could speak of, she did occasionally reject potential renters for moral reasons.

Police have since stated that they know who committed the murder, but that they have no physical evidence tying the suspect to the crime, and therefore cannot pursue prosecution unless new evidence comes to light.

For your consideration:

~ According to an *Argus Leader* article, authorities twice visited Texas to interview a suspect. Might that suspect still be alive and living in Texas? Does this suspect have ties to South Dakota?

~ Strangulation, like a stabbing or other close-contact physical assault, is a personal, anger-driven crime. Might someone who was angry Clara wouldn't rent to him or her have committed this crime? Did Clara know her attacker?

If you know anything about this crime, please contact Sioux Falls Police Department at (605)-367-7212 To submit an anonymous tip, contact CrimeStoppers at (605)-367-7007.

Photo courtesy of <u>Argus Leader</u>
(Ref: *Argus Leader; KELO News*)

Stanley Strole
Missing Person

Stanley Strole was 37 years old when he disappeared on March 15, 1979. He was last seen at the Palm Gardens Bar in Aberdeen, SD.

Stanley is white, about 6' tall, 150 pounds, with brown eyes and short dark brown/black hair. He has a burn scar on his shoulder. Stanley is a Type 1 diabetic and left his insulin behind when he disappeared. There's no information on what he was wearing at the time he went missing, but he usually wore button-up shirts, slacks with a belt, and dress shoes.

According to an article in the *Aberdeen News*, Aberdeen, SD, Stanley had gotten into an argument with his sister because she would not buy him beer due to his diabetes. He then left the house, went to the bank, withdrew all his money from his account and went to the Palm Gardens.

He was not reported missing until June of 1979, according to Aberdeen Police Dept reports. In 1986, an officer of the Aberdeen Police Department interviewed his sister, Vicki Opp, who told him that Stanley often threatened to run away, and told him about Stanley's argument with another sister. She stated that she had heard from a Palm Gardens employee that Stanley had shown up at the Palm Gardens and began flashing his money around and drinking beer. When police questioned this employee, he told the officer that isn't what he'd said.

In later police interviews, Vicki Opp added that Stanley had gotten into a red pickup with three other men.

He hasn't been seen since, and DNA from his family is on file, if an unidentified body matching his description is found. All four sisters, his only siblings, have passed away.

For your consideration:
~ If Stanley had his own bank account and access to it, why did he need his sister to buy him beer?
~ Why would a simple thing, like his sister's refusal to buy him beer, cause him to react in such a rash way? Was Stanley dealing with an alcohol issue, which led to his disappearance and possible ultimate demise?
~ Why would the Palm Gardens employee tell police he never made those statements about Stanley showing his money around, when Vicki Opp told police several times he had?

If you know any details about the disappearance of Stanley Strole, please contact the Aberdeen Police Department at (605) 626-7000.

(Ref: *Aberdeen News*, Sept 18, 2021)

Leone & Stanley Strole
About 1945

Stanley Strole was born September 29, 1941, to Leo and Thelma Strole. He was later joined by five sisters: Leone, Cleo, Vicki, Kathy, and Connie.

Stanley lived on his own, having never married or had children.

Kelly Day, Stanley's niece, was nine years old when he went missing. Although she doesn't remember much about him, she does recall that he loved fishing, was kind, playful, and enjoyed his nieces and nephews, doling out quarters when he saw them. And most of all, she remembers how he was and is loved and missed.

Kelly has taken up the torch in pursuit of his whereabouts.
*Photos courtesy of Kelly Day

Eugene Luverne "Beaner" Prins
Missing Person

On the evening of March 26, 2020, Eugene "Beaner" Prins walked out of Doren's Bar in Forestburg, SD. Security footage of him leaving approximately 7:38 p.m. on that Thursday evening is the last verifiable sighting of him.

Earlier in the day, Eugene had withdrawn $350.00 from the bank and had purchased $130 worth of groceries. He had hung out with his friend, Dan, the majority of the day, and later that evening at the bar. Eugene left his Ford Escape parked at his home that day and presumably rode with Dan.

Some witnesses state that shortly before Beaner left the

bar, he and Dan had a discussion about leaving; Beaner wanted to leave and Dan did not. It didn't appear that either man was overly intoxicated. Shortly after Beaner walked out, Dan walked out.

Dan states that he gave Eugene a ride when they left the bar, and they drove to another friend's house. Since Eugene was asleep in the car, Dan entered the home alone. This farm was located on a gravel road in rural Woonsocket, around six miles away from Forestburg. He claims he was in the home for about 20 minutes, and when he came back out, Eugene was gone. He initiated a search on his own, but having no luck, Dan called his wife to come help him. Still no luck.

About 9:10 p.m., Dan drove to town to tell Eugene's brothers that Eugene was missing. The brothers, not believing Dan was serious, went on with their work. But the next morning, when no one had seen Eugene, Dan called Jeff, Eugene's mother's partner, to tell him Eugene was missing. Authorities were notified, and official searches began with search teams through law enforcement, Mitchell Dive and Water Rescue, Mitchell Search and Rescue, walkers, horses, ATVs, 4-wheelers, planes, and helicopters. Local farms, outbuildings, groves, ravines, creeks, drainage ditches, and overgrown areas were searched, but no trace of Eugene was found.

Later, two witnesses, young men in the area, came forward and claim to have seen Eugene, or someone matching his description, walking south from that farm, about 100 yards away, at about 8:30 p.m. Footprints, believed to be Eugene's, were found on the road, but stopped abruptly.

The weather that day was relatively mild: around 40 degrees, with little snow left on the ground.

In the months and years that followed, multiple searches for Eugene in the way of drones, cadaver dogs, search teams, kayakers, and The Prairie Patriots Water Search Team have been employed but yielded no results. In a later search, cadaver dogs hit on four bales of hay nearby, but nothing was found linking Eugene to those bales.

Eugene was last seen wearing a gray hooded shirt, blue plaid coat and gray stocking hat, light khaki pants, and tennis shoes. Eugene has dark, graying hair and a beard, wears dark-rimmed glasses, and has a tattoo of his nickname, "Beaner" on his right arm. Both his ears are pierced, and he is missing some teeth. He is 5'7" and weighs approximately 170 pounds, and has brown eyes. He was born May 14, 1974, and was 45 years of age at the time of his disappearance.

Eugene left behind a loving family, a host of friends, and beloved pet, a lab-pit mix named Shadow.

For your consideration:

~ With the weather as mild as it was, it's unlikely that Beaner walked off and tried to seek protection elsewhere. Why wouldn't he remain in Dan's car? Was he tired of waiting, or did he wake up and not know where he was and wandered off? How intoxicated was he? Was he asleep or passed out?

If Beaner had wandered off on his own and passed out in a ditch somewhere, he would have been found by now, which is highly suggestive of foul play. Did someone pick him up and rob him? And if so, why wouldn't they drop him off, or (worst case), dump him somewhat nearby?

~ What would anyone have to gain by abducting a man who, by all accounts, had no enemies, posed no threat, and, other than the approximately $220 he had *before* drinks, had nothing of real value on his person?

~ What if Dan had been mistaken in his time spent inside his friend's home? Then again, he *did* make it back to Forestburg by 9:10 p.m. to tell Eugene's brothers he was missing.

~ The last known sighting of Beaner was on security camera footage outside Doren's bar. Was he seen getting into Dan's car? Why would Dan come forward and admit to giving Beaner a ride if there was no proof of him being with Beaner when he left the bar?

~ Were the kids mistaken about the time they saw the man on the road, or did they maybe see Dan looking for Eugene?

If you know anything about the disappearance of Eugene "Beaner" Prins, please contact the Sanborn County Sheriff's Office at (605) 796-4511

Or SD DCI at (605) 773-3331.

(Ref: *Mitchell Republic*; Pat Scholtes,)

Eugene "Beaner" Prins

Every day since his disappearance, Eugene's mother, Pat, posts a public letter to him on Facebook. Some days, she fills him in on recent local events. But most, she laments her loss of him and its unbearable toll on her heart.

March 30, 2020
The start of day four my nightmare continues. Beaner was—no, is—my first born, my one child that was just mine, no father in his life, so I didn't have to share him with anyone. That makes for a very special bond. I always believed I was strong.

And I'm trying to be for my other three kids, but this, this has brought me to my knees. I would do anything I could for any of them and they know that.

I need my son back...my heart will never be whole again... we need to find him - my family is hurting so much right now.

Mother's Day, 2021:

It's day 409, son, and my second Mothers Day without you. And it's no easier than last year. It looks like it will be just Jeff and I this year. I miss you even more on days like this; after all you made me a mother for the first time. I knew then I wanted more children. I never knew I could love someone as much as I love all of you. There is nothing I wouldn't do for any of you to keep you save and loved.

Now I sit here and go over memories of past Mother's Days when you were all here with me. I miss those good days you know. I would give anything for you to be here with me again. I may not know where you are son but I love you just as much as I ever have and nothing will ever change that.

When we were out yesterday I think I was on the verge of tears the whole time. It just seemed so hopeless, like what am I even looking for now. I know I'm not going to find the beautiful young man that left here that night a year ago. But I can't seem to find anything. And that's what hurts the most.

I miss you son I just want you home. I love you so much son we all do. I love you Beaner Always and Forever.

March 26th, 2022:

I don't even know where to start this morning son. I have been awake since two but forced myself to stay in bed as long as I could. I did not want to get up and have to face this day. But I finally had no choice. It wasn't going to go away no matter what I did.

It's day 730 for us son, it's officially been two years today since I've seen you or was able to have contact of any kind with you. And it has most definitely been the worst two years of my life.

My emotions are all over the place this morning, I don't

know if I want to scream, get angry or just sit here and cry. At this point any of them could happen.

Do you suppose anyone else is having memories with you just flooding their minds this morning. Or do you suppose they have forgotten all about you too after all the memory of what happened that night conveniently disappeared. How does that even happen anyway, that night and what really happened has been blocked out for a reason.

I think about you all the time, not a minute passes that you are not on my mind. I treasure every moment of our lives we were allowed to be together. Being your mother is one of the greatest honors I could have been given son. You have always given me so much joy all your life. And still do today it's just different now.

I was an eighteen year old single mother when you were born. And it wasn't always easy for us but you were so perfect that any struggle we had to deal with was so worth it just to have you in my arms. Who knew a little four and a half pound little boy would change my life forever. But it did, and it was all for the good son. You will always be the light of my life.

I miss you so much Beaner, my heart is breaking right now from missing you. And yes the tears have started and I don't know if I can stop them today. You were taken from us for no possible reason. Why did this happen son, why am I fighting just to make it through every single day in one piece.

This pain is never going to end until you are found and back home with us. I just hope it's soon because the last two years have been pure hell for all of us here.

I love you son Always and Forever
Pat Scholtes, Eugene's mother

*Photos courtesy of Pat Scholtes

Beaner,

There are so many things that were left unsaid, if only we could bring you home. The years keep ticking by and we have zero information. How can that be? Where did you go? Who did this to you? We think we know, yet we don't know. We continue to hope, pray, look for answers anywhere there might possibly be some and still . . . nothing. The one thing we are grateful for is all the wonderful memories that we have with you. Nobody can take that away from us.

Easter just passed and I was thinking of all those Easter weekends we spent together when you were in Minnesota. That was a big deal for us. We would sit around with these HUGE Easter baskets and all of us would go through them to see what was all there and trade back and forth. Time has gone so fast, Bean. What we wouldn't give to relive those moments. I wonder if we knew then what we know now, would we have treasured those moments more or are they more treasured now because we didn't know how important they would be then? I guess it doesn't matter, does it? Those moments are like gold to us now.

All the summers we spent together at grannies. Why anyone thought we should oversee watching Timmy and Becky is beyond me, but we kept them safe and for the most part, none of us got into trouble . . . well, what they don't know won't hurt them, right? Granny sure had her hands full with us, though, didn't she? Those summers were the best. We would ride our bikes everywhere. Remember when the little ice cream shop was right down the street from Grandma's? We would get those little cones with the crunch topping on them. We loved those.

When we'd go "fishing" at the lake and all the little sunfish were right at the end of the bridge and we'd try to catch them.

We'd spend hours doing that.

We used to do so many things together. We'd write letters back and forth and see who could write in the smallest print; you won every single time. All those bike trips we took to the fireworks stands. Taking our $1 from Grandma and going to the IGA to get our glass bottle of soda and all the penny candy we could get and sitting outside and enjoying our treats. All the conversations we had about growing up, what we would do, where we would go, finding a wife and a husband, having our families grow up together. You and I both wanted kids and it just never worked out for either of us. There must have been a reason, right? All our shenanigans growing up, sometimes I'm surprised we did make it through our teenage years. The bridge incident, I don't know if we ever told anyone about that. I still can't do tuna noodle helper, either, lol.

We had so many good times together and we had some not so good times, too, but we know we loved each other. We grew up together, we were our first best friends. You were the first grandson, and I was the first granddaughter, and we are only five months apart. Beaner, I miss you. I'm sorry for all those things that were left between us.

The memories are all any of us have left. You know what? That's not entirely true. You left more than your memories with us. All of us have some part of you with us in our hearts, in our minds, in our souls. You are more than a memory, Beaner, you are way more than just a memory. You are a son, a brother, a nephew, a grandson, an uncle, a friend, and most importantly, to me you are my cousin who was more like a brother.

Whoever took you from us, they have that memory to live with and they will have to answer to someone, someday. As a family, we hope we see that day. The life they took, the future they stole, will not be forgotten and we won't let it.

Bean, I love you. I think of you every single day. You are not forgotten and never will be. We will fight to our last breath to bring you home.

All my love, Sara

Happy Birthday, brother. I miss you more then you can imagine. Just everyday, I sit and wonder, "why you?" Why the guy who would give anyone the shirt off his back if he knew it could help them more then himself? The guy who never held a grudge and forgave and forgave, even to those that wronged him the most. Why you? Why our family?

I hope when I get to your age, Bean, I'm at least half the man that you are. You are one of my idols; always have been. You don't realize how much it meant to me to have you at both my college and high school graduations. How much those little insignificant chats we had when I was barely awake and you were leaving mom's, after you ate, meant to me.

You and Tim have done so much to shape my entire life. Tim has shown me how to be father and how to put in the work to make the best out of crappy situation. But you, Bean, you showed me more then anyone how to be a caring person in a world that don't care about people. You taught me to work hard for everything, and no matter what life throws at you there's no sense in crying about it. You just go and do what you can. I love you more then you can ever imagine, Bean. I always will.

Love, your Big Little Brother Colton

East Lee
Unsolved Death

On October 20, 2015, a pheasant hunter, scouting in the area of Brueschke Lake near Eagle Butte, stumbled upon the body of 19-year-old East Lee. He'd been shot in the head and left where he fell.

His mother knew something was wrong when she hadn't gotten a call or text from her son for two days. The phone call from the FBI confirmed her worst fears: someone had murdered her son.

East Lee had been struggling with meth addiction but had recently gotten clean and was ready for a change. He'd planned to move away to continue his education and get a job, but it didn't happen soon enough. He was murdered before he could make those changes.

Growing up, East had been involved with any kind of sport he could find. He enjoyed boxing and basketball when he was very young and then got involved with track, basketball, and football in upper grades.

But once meth got its grips in him, he fell in with the wrong crowd, and that association haunted him into adulthood.

Very little is known about the events leading up to the shooting that claimed East Lee's life, and his family and law enforcement are desperate for answers. East left behind a young son, his parents, and a host of loving family and friends.

The FBI previously offered a $5,000 reward, which the Cheyenne River Sioux Tribe agreed to match, increasing the total reward to $10,000 for information leading to the arrest and conviction of those responsible for the death of Lee.

For your consideration:

~ Was East's past association with drug dealers or a drug cartel responsible for his death?

~ What possible motive would they have to kill East, given his recent break from meth? Was he a threat? Did he know too much?

If you know anything about the murder of East Lee, please contact the
Minneapolis Field Office of the FBI at (763) 569-8000
Or FBI Pierre Resident Agency at (605) 224-1331
Or submit anonymous tips to tips.fbi.gov.

(Ref: *KELOLAND News; KOTA Territory News*)

This is my son, East Lee. He was 19 years old when he was shot in the head and left for dead in a field. My son was a father, a brother, and takoja (grandson) to many.

He was the kid who drove you around for hours and hours so you didn't kill yourself (one man's story). He would take you to our home and feed you, give you some shoes because your girlfriend threw yours away. He was the kid who reminded me daily that I am not to judge anyone because I wasn't God. My son was Sundancer and believed in the Lakota way of life. He had strong spirit who everyone says "the kids gravitated to him."

He attended high school at Cheyenne Eagle Butte and graduated in 2014, he was part of the State A basketball team for CEB.

Every household goes through addiction or problems, and on the Rez, it's alcohol or drugs. Recently back in 2012, meth was brought in and it's taken over our community, our land, our people, and even our leaders. We can't say our kids won't do that because obviously it happens to even the richest sanest families. Meth and money play a role and so do our relatives. I say relatives because as Lakota people "we are all related." Many have been indicted, banished and some dead since my son's murder.

My son deserves justice and we, as family, deserve closure.
Sherri Turning Heart

*Photo courtesy of Sherri Turning Heart

Journey of Unknowns

This book is comprised of unsolved cases dating back to 1969, though it is not comprehensive. Without enough information to share, some had to be omitted or slated for a possible second book. Some of the cases I found only supplied a name and unsolved cause of death or disappearance, but lacking more information, I had to omit them. And a few are omitted because a family requested his or her loved one's case not be included.

Throughout this journey of unknowns in the writing of this book, I've found that the older the case, the more likely those left behind tend to find peace with it. Like the fear of hope has overcome hope itself.

Does it mean the search for justice or answers has ended? Does it mean that those mothers, fathers, siblings, and children no longer seek resolution or peace? No. But that the ebb and flow of grief and hope and desperation and peaceful resignation is just that: ebb and flow. It's the fluctuating current, even cascading waves, that takes a toll, not the grief, hope, desperation, and peaceful resignation. The stirring up of all those is now the crux of their enduring pain, not simply the loss.

That is not to say they are choosing to forget their loved one. Far from it. They're choosing to remember their loved one apart from the tragedy that stole them away. They're choosing peace.

Most of us will never know the excruciating trauma of losing someone to murder or disappearance. I've learned through this project that sometimes, there is a stillness in pain; that it isn't always writhing, wailing, and clenching of teeth. Sometimes it's breathing through it, calming the churning surges of agony, and focusing on the future moment when that surge is over and the lull of peace is found.

Grief is universal. Each and every person's reaction to grief is not. It's a journey of unknowns.

Ladonna, Brian, and Patrick Mathis Unsolved Deaths

At 4 a.m. on September 8, 1981, authorities received a call from John Mathis in rural Mount Vernon, SD. He stated that someone had shot his family and to send an ambulance.

Authorities arrived at the farm and went to the machine shed where the Mathis family had been sleeping while their house was being rebuilt.

John and Ladonna also had a nine-month-old son, Duane, who was too young to sleep in the chilly shed. He was staying with her parents.

They found Ladonna, 30, and their two sons, 4-year-old Brian, and 2-year-old Patrick, dead in their beds. Ladonna had been shot twice in the head at close range, apparently while she slept. Brian had been shot once in the right ear. Patrick had been shot in the back of the neck and in the left eye, and later reports would state that he had been kneeling when the second shot killed him.

John Mathis, in pain but subdued, was also shot in the left arm. He claimed that Patrick had woken him up because he needed to go to the bathroom. He took Patrick outside, and while there, he heard one of his hogs in distress. He returned Patrick to his bed, and went out to check on the pig. He then tied up the family dog and heard a car, and saw that the lights were on in the machine shed where his family was sleeping.

He went on to claim that a masked intruder exited the shed and the two got into a scuffle, John got shot in the arm, and he then passed out. When he came to, the intruder was gone. He checked on his family, found they had been shot, and called authorities. Mathis stated that the intruder had spray-painted the words, "Mathus sucks" (Mathis' name spelled incorrectly) on the sliding door of the shed before fleeing.

At the hospital where John's gunshot wound was being treated, officers discover a live .22 caliber Winchester bullet in John's pocket, but John claimed that Patrick had found it on the ground and handed it to him earlier in the day. He stated the shells were everywhere on his farm.

The Davison County Sheriff's Office led the search for the murder weapon, a .22 caliber semi-automatic Marlin using Winchester Western Super X bullets. Though several .22 caliber rifles were sent to the crime lab in Pierre, none matched the bullets that killed the family. All buildings on the farm, including the sewage pit under the hog facility, and fields nearby, were searched extensively in an effort to find the murder weapon. None was ever found.

SD DCI and the FBI also coordinated efforts to find information about the murders.

John Mathis became the lead suspect in the case, and authorities questioned whether his father might be involved, as John's father was approaching the Mathis house just as law enforcement officials were arriving, and stopped questioning of John in the hospital, forcing law enforcement to leave the room.

Deputy Sheriff Doug Kirkus stated in an article that he felt something was "off" when he began questioning John about the events of that night. One claim John made to Kirkus was that the masked intruder attacked him outside the shed, but blood was only found inside the shed, not outside.

Adding to the suspicions of John Mathis' involvement

in the murders was the two previous fires on the farm. On July 9th at 2:30 a.m., Ladonna awoke to a fire in the house, and quickly got out with her children, only to find John already outside working. The second fire, July 22nd, consumed the house.

That fall, a Davison County grand jury indicted John Mathis on three counts of first-degree murder. The trial began in April of 1982, and in order to avoid a biased jury, the trial was moved to Yankton.

The trial went on for a month. The defense claimed that the bullet in Mathis' pants pocket was not unusual, that .22 bullets were everywhere. In an eerie twist, later when the trial was wrapping up, a juror leaving the trial found a .22 Winchester Super X shell bullet outside on the sidewalk directly in front of the courthouse.

The defense stated that bullets like that are commonplace, found everywhere, adding credence to the discovery of the bullet in front of the courthouse as well as their defense strategy. The prosecution felt that the bullet was planted to give just that impression.

Prosecution had no witnesses, no weapon, and very little physical evidence tying John to the murders. In May of 1982, John Mathis was acquitted.

Duane, who had been in the care of Ladonna's parents, was returned to John Mathis after his acquittal, and Ladonna's parents never saw him again.

For your consideration:
~ What, if anything, could law enforcement have done differently in the investigation? Did they check John's vehicle to see if it had been driven recently (warm to the touch)?
~ Double jeopardy prohibits John Mathis from ever

being tried in the murders again. (It does not prohibit John Mathis from being charged in other charges related to the case, should any evidence turn up.) Why did the state choose to try him for all three murders, rather than one? Wouldn't that have given them the opportunity to seek another trial at a later date if more evidence turned up?

~ How did the bullet get on the sidewalk in front of the courthouse at the end of the trial?

~ What motive would John have to murder his family?

~ What, if anything, can be made of the suspicious fires at the house just before the shooting deaths?

If you know anything about the murders of Ladonna, Brian, and Patrick Mathis, please contact the Davison County Sheriff's Office at (605) 995-8639

Or the SD DCI at (605) 773-3331

Or the FBI at (605) 334-6881

Or to submit an anonymous tip, call Mitchell CrimeStoppers at (605) 996-1700

(Ref: *Mitchell Republic; KELOLAND News*; Trail Went Cold Podcast, Marilyn Reimnitz)

Ladonna Mathis

Brian and Patrick Mathis

Ladonna was born October 8, 1950. She grew up in a loving Christian home and sent to grades 1-8 in a rural country a school one mile from home. Ladonna was baptized and confirmed at Immanuel Lutheran church rural Dimock, SD.

Ladonna played piano and took lessons from a close

neighbor. Ladonna taught me how to play piano and we would play duets. She had no prom dates but was happy to be with friends who also did not have dates. She graduated from Corsica High School in 1968.

Ladonna didn't go to college but was hired by Corsica public school as business manager for a short time. She then was employed by National Bank of S.D. and enjoyed working with people and the business aspect for 4 years. After only a short time of employment, she was promoted to first teller and more responsibility. She had beautiful thick dark brown hair.

She was excellent in sewing her own clothes and when the town of Mitchell stores would be open till 9pm on Monday nights she would shop. She took pride in her first car, a 1964 blue Chevy Impala. While earning her own money, Ladonna bought a bedroom set and a stereo.

She had several boyfriends and would go to Milltown and Dimock dances. She met John in Mitchell, SD, and I am not sure where or how they met. They had a 2-year courtship. What drew her to John was maybe because he had his own farm and was a hard worker. He did not smoke nor drink or stay out to 4 in the morning to party. They were married May 4, 1973. John was not a churchgoer, but she did get him to go on occasion.

Thru Ladonna's business knowledge, the farm they lived on got paid off. She raised and butchered her own chickens. Ladonna loved her 3 boys and they were close together in age so that made for a busy mother. Brian couldn't speak well so she took him for speech therapy. Brian and Patrick 's lives were taken before they could even start living. Brian enjoyed riding his trike as I had the honor of riding a bigger bike with him around their yard. Patrick was an active 2 year old. Ladonna kept them well clothed and never with out shoes.

From Marilyn Reimnitz, Ladonna's sister
*Photos courtesy of Marilyn Reimnitz

Robert LueVerne Odman
Missing Person

Robert Odman disappeared from Sioux Falls, SD, in September of 1995 after an altercation with his two sons. He left a note, got into his silver Chevy Blazer, and left. His son, Chris, stated that he didn't remember exactly what the note said, only that it was somewhat of a goodbye letter.

Robert's Blazer was later found abandoned on the interstate near the Hartford, SD, exit, but no trace of Robert was found.

His family feels the death of his 26-year-old daughter, Michelle, from cancer hit him particularly hard, as it had the entire family. After her death, his life had spiraled; he had split with his wife, had lost his job, and in a final blow, had a falling out with his sons. One of Robert's sons has since died.

On January 6th, 1996, Robert resurfaced in Walsenburg, CO, at a police station, and asked where the local homeless shelter was. He walked out and has not been seen since. However, some online reports claim he arrived at the homeless shelter, and told them that he wanted to be left alone.

His son states that Robert may not be in hiding or may not even know he is considered missing; he may just be staying away of his own accord. After this many years, though, they are left to wonder if he met with foul play, as he hasn't been in touch with anyone in his family, even after the death of his son. The family would still like to find him, if possible.

Robert is Caucasian, has sandy brown hair, blue eyes, and is approximately 6'2" and 175-190 pounds. He was born on September 29, 1942, and was 53 years of age when he went missing.

He is blind in the left eye, has a scar on his abdomen, and a tattoo on his forearm of a knife with a skull.

For your consideration:
~ Why would Robert abandon his vehicle? Did it break down or run out of gas?
~ How did he reach Colorado?
~ Did he have any money to travel? Why abandon a vehicle that would be a means of gaining some money?
~ Did Robert decide to permanently disappear or has something nefarious happened to Robert?
~ What did the note say?

If you know something about the disappearance of Robert Odman, please contact the Sioux Falls Police Department at (605) 367-7000.
Photo courtesy of Chris Odman
(Ref: The Charley Project, the Odman Family)

Where are you, Dad? Why did you leave? Even after so many years, I still grieve for you. You've no idea what you've missed. I'd like to think you're nearby, watching us, keeping track of our lives, but if that were so, how could you stay away, seeing your own son pass away and not be here to grieve with us?

You've missed the birth of grandchildren, and now great grandchildren. Don't you want to know them? My oldest misses her papa. I miss you. I was your little girl. I remember my spot in the car, right behind you, every single time we went away together. I remember wanting you to be the first to know I was expecting again. I remember how you and Mom supported me when I needed your help. Not everything I recall is good. But I'm learning to choose those good memories over the bad. For me.

Dad, I know you. I know you struggled with alcohol, but I also know how very resourceful and strong you are. Maybe you're out there, living a different life away from the pain of losing our sister, your daughter. I know that was hard. It was hard for us, too. But if leaving was your way of grieving, why didn't you come back? And if you met up with someone who harmed you, I hope you found peace.

We needed you then, but we need you still. I want to know why. I want to know where you are! But mostly, I want you back. I miss you.

Darcy Odman

Cody Ray Rodriguez
South Dakota Ties
Unsolved Death
Closed without Closure

On September 10, 2008, 1:30 a.m., Ina Mae Rodriguez answered a phone call from her niece, Ashley. "Auntie Mae! They say Cody killed himself. He shot himself in the back of his head!"

Cody Ray Rodriguez lived in Salt Lake City, Utah, at apartment #327, 880 Oak Tree Lane. When authorities and paramedics arrived, they found Cody inside the door to his apartment with a gunshot wound to his head, lying in a puddle of blood.

Police interviewed the only witness, Kenneth Mark Anderson, who claimed that Cody was staying with him and had just arrived home just as Mr. Anderson was stepping outside to have a cigarette. He stated that right after he exited the apartment, Cody suddenly shot himself inside the door of the residence. Mr. Anderson said he placed a towel underneath Cody's head.

According to information provided to private investigators, police entered the apartment, finding Cody with his head near the door, feet leading toward the living room. They discovered a weapon, a silver .357 Magnum, between his left arm and his upper body. They moved the weapon to a counter top for safety reasons as paramedics worked on Cody.

Cody was transported to a nearby hospital where he died. His death was ruled a suicide.

Ina Mae, however, didn't believe it. Before she'd left Salt

Lake to return to SD, Cody told his mother, "Mama, I'm going back to school and I'm going to buy us a house." Those were the last words she'd heard from him.

The next day, Ina Mae called the detective in charge of the case and asked for the medical examiner's number. She called the M.E. and asked if there was gunpowder residue on Cody's hands. He stated he had not seen soot, gunpowder stippling, or other visible residues of weapon discharge on Cody's hands at the time of his examination, and released a statement to her stating the same. She stated that she begged him not to close the case with a determination of suicide, but he said that unless the authorities told him otherwise, he would have to close it as a suicide.

From the outset of her investigation into her son's death, Ina Mae encountered numerous inconsistencies, conflicting evidence, and rumors contrary to the police's finding of suicide. Sgt. Brandon Shearer, a spokesman for Salt Lake City Police stated they'd conducted several investigations with the same conclusion: it was suicide. He stated three detectives conducted separate investigations beginning in 2010, and an independent review conducted by investigators with the district attorney's office, who also confirmed the findings of the police department.

Police also stated another investigation took place after the medical examiner sent the letter to Ina Mae, and again, the findings pointed to suicide. They said if there is new information or if the medical examiner reaches a different conclusion, they will re-open the case.

"TO WHOM IT MAY CONCERN"

On October, 28, 2015, the Utah Department of Health, Office of the Medical Examiner, sent a letter to Ina Mae Rodriguez stating:

"Re: OME case 200801411, RODRIGUEZ, C

To Whom It May Concern:

At the request of Ms. Ina Mae Rodriguez, I am writing to confirm that no evidence of soot, gunpowder stippling or other visible residues of weapon discharge was seen on the hands of the decedent when examined at the Utah Office of Medical Examiner at 0945 on 9/10/2008.
(Signed)
Todd C. Grey, MD
Chief Medical Examiner"

This document seems to dispute the findings of suicide in Cody's death. While it is not proof that Cody did not fire the gun, and does not disclose forensic test findings, if they were done at all, it adds to the mystery that a Chief Medical Examiner could not see visible evidence to support the argument that Cody fired the gun.
BLOOD TRAIL:
In evidence supplied by authorities to Ina Mae's private investigators, photos show a blood trail, presumably Cody's blood, down the corridor between four apartments from unit #326 to #327. The following information is from Jensen Private Investigations: Outside the doorway of unit #326 was a pool of blood, indicating the victim was

stationary long enough for the blood to pool. The blood trail shimmies left and right, and is inconsistent in pooling, suggesting periods of cessation of forward movement, as if the victim were being carried. The pattern, had the victim been ambulatory, forward facing, and upright, would have been on the right leading to the place where the victim had been found. The relative placement of his blood trail was on the left, as if the victim were carried face up from one apartment to the other, where he was found. Statements from the witness did not include any details about the victim being moved or moving himself from place to place. Evidence suggests the victim was moved from one location to the location where he was found, but no reports given to Ina Mae indicate any police interviews of the occupants of #326, nor were any photos taken inside that residence.

THE SHOES:

Since Cody's death in 2008, Ina Mae had been provided two pair of shoes, with claims that both pairs were shoes worn by the decedent. In the Body Inventory & Release Sheet, it's documented that Mrs. Rodriguez picked up her son's personal effects, including a pair of shoes the victim had been wearing at the time he was autopsied. However, later, in April of 2013, Mrs. Rodriguez picked up "evidence" collected from the scene, which included a pair of shoes that had been documented in photos of the scene, but collected after the victim had been removed from the scene. These were not Cody's shoes; Cody was wearing shoes when he left the scene and when he was autopsied. Blood is found on only the right shoe of the second pair, and the pattern in which it flowed onto the shoe is significant: it flowed from the top, and trickled down the sides of the shoe, as if spilled or dripped onto the top of the foot of someone who was upright while wearing it. There was no blood found on the left shoe.

THE WITNESS:

In photos taken of the witness after the shooting, the witness' hands contained blood, more so the right hand, presumably from putting the victim's head on the towel. There did not appear to be velocity blood present on the witness' hands. The witness was also shown in photos to be in his stocking feet, not wearing shoes at the time he is interviewed by authorities.

THE BLOOD:

In several photos of the scene taken after the victim was removed from the residence, what appears to be diluted blood is present on the bathroom door inside the apartment #327, on the kitchen sink backsplash, as well as on a toilet paper roll in the bathroom drawer. No explanation of the presence of blood on these surfaces is ever addressed.

THE GUN:

In the two reports provided to Ina Mae Rodriguez, details about the gun are not discussed. From the photos, it is clear that the gun is a Ruger SP101 .357 Magnum, serial #572-07494. The gunshot caused a penetrating wound, i.e. there was no exit wound. There were no reports provided stating who owned the gun, nor were any provided stating whether finger or palm prints were ordered or acquired or attempted from the gun to determine who fired the shot. In evidence photos taken by authorities, velocity blood is clearly present on the weapon, and in one photo, the blood spot appears to be diluted. After the case was deemed suicide and the case closed, the gun was returned to the owner.

CODY:

While the medical examiner did issue a written statement to Ina Mae that "no evidence of soot, gunpowder stippling, or other visible weapon discharge was seen on the hands of the decedent when examined at the Utah Office of Medical Examiner at 0945 on 9/10/2008," she said police informed her that a gunshot residue test would not be conducted. She said they told her it was too costly, and that the process was not reliable. However, the victim's hands were bagged, as shown in evidence photos, as if testing was intended. It's uncertain if testing was in fact done and no reports were shared with her, or if they were not done at all.

THE PLACEMENT OF THE GUN:

When officers arrived on the scene, the first to find Cody described finding the gun near Mr. Rodriguez, between his left arm and his body as he lay face up. The officer says he moved the gun to the countertop for safety reasons. Two reports are provided to Ina Mae, neither of which address the details surrounding ownership or chain of custody of the gun, or its history in a crime. Officer Angeline Portel reported, "Officers J. Miller and N. Schnieder arrived first at Mr. Anderson's apartment. They assisted me in booking the handgun into evidence." Officer Schnieder reported, "A silver handgun (was) lying next to his body. The gun was lying between his left arm and his body." The placement of the gun has led Ina Mae and her private investigator to question the assumption of suicide. Ina Mae's private investigator report states: "According to Barry A. J. Fisher, Crime Lab Director of the Los Angeles County Sheriff's Office, 'In suicides involving handguns, the victim usually drops the weapon or throws it up to several feet away when the arms are flung outward.' Fisher stated that floors should be examined for dents or scratches because of this phenomenon, but no reports are found saying if officers did check for dents or scratches. The gun was a .357 Magnum, which are known for substantial recoil. This should have resulted in the gun being thrown in a direction opposite to the trajectory of the bullet's path. Fisher also stated that occasionally, a gun used in suicide is found in the hand of the decedent, but it's usually due to the gun or hand having been supported or propped at the time of discharge. In this incidence, it does not suggest any possibility of propping. The gun being thrown or dropped to the right of the body would be more consistent with suicide, but the gun was found on the left."

For your consideration:
~ Who was wearing the second pair of shoes, and how did Cody's blood get on them? Why only the right shoe and not the left? Why did they get sent home with Cody's belongings when Ina Mae picked them up?

~ Regarding the blood dripped on the right shoe of the second pair of shoes given to Ina Mae: if the person wearing them had been standing still, wouldn't blood also likely splash onto the left? Is it conceivable that the person wearing these shoes would have had to be in motion in order for it not to splash onto the left?

~ Is it customary to release evidence back to the family if there's even a shred of doubt or questions as to the manner of death? If more details regarding Cody's death emerge, isn't the evidence given to Ina Mae now inadmissible, having lost its chain of custody?

~ Was fingerprint analysis done or attempted on the gun?

~ Was gunpowder residue testing ever done on Cody's hands, as implied by the bagging of Cody's hands? Why are there no reports regarding whether or not this was done? Were Cody's roommate's hands ever tested?

~ Whose decision is it to determine "manner of death"? Is it the medical examiner or the police? In one statement, the medical examiner claims that unless the authorities told him otherwise, he had to close it as a suicide. And police state that if the medical examiner "reaches a different conclusion," they would re-open the case. Who is in charge of re-opening the case?

~ How could Cody fire a gun and not have visible evidence of gunpowder stippling or residue on his hands?

~ Why is there no mention of any interviews of the occupants of apartment #326, where the blood trail seemed to originate? Why is there no record of any photos being taken in this apartment, especially given the blood trail that clearly connects Cody to it?

~ Was there ever any question as to Cody's manner of death, or did officials simply take the witness' word for it, and proceed without doubt? Is this typical in all suspected suicides?

~ Why are there no reports as to who the gun was registered to? How did Cody get it? Why was it returned rather than kept in evidence?

~ Was there an examination of Cody's brain to determine the path of the bullet? Wouldn't the trajectory of the bullet help determine whether it was fired from right to left (if Cody had fired the gun) or from back to front (if someone else had fired it)?

~ Were autopsy reports released to the family? If this is indeed a closed case, can the family seek the release of these findings?

~ Can another, independent autopsy be done to do more extensive tests?

If you know anything about the death of Cody Ray Rodriguez, please contact

Salt Lake City Police Department at (801) 799-3000

Or submit an anonymous tip by texting TIPSLCPD and your info to 274-637

Or call in an anonymous tip to (801) 799-4636

Or submit an anonymous tip to Salt Lake City CrimeStoppers at (801) 964-2255.

(Ref: *Salt Lake City's ABC4-Utah News*; Jensen Private Investigations; Ina Mae Rodriguez)

I miss my son so much. It still hurts every day. I pray I never forget his loving hugs and kisses.

My son loved life, and most of all he loved us, his family. He was very much a mamma's boy. Cody Ray loved life and his family, although Cody wanted to stay behind in Salt Lake City, Utah, with his friends. He always called me to tell me, "Mom, I love you. I'm going back to school so I can get us a house, and we can all live together again." He was looking to get his GED so he can get into massage therapy in Vegas. He loved basketball and his friends, but one thing he didn't like is when his friends would come against one another.

My son had the kindest heart. He used to bring his friends home to eat or sleep over. He was the only one who always told me, "Momma, I love you," with a kiss on my cheek.

Ina Mae Rodriguez

First off, I would like to start off by saying how caring and loving Cody Ray was. He was my protector, and had a heart of gold. He loved his family to the fullest. Growing up with Cody Ray, we were very close. He was always thinking of others before himself. It breaks my heart to know it's been years since he's been gone, and my family still has no closure. He is thought of daily and will never be forgotten.

Ashley Rodriguez, Cody's cousin

*Photo courtesy of Ina Mae Rodriguez

Beverly Ulrich
Missing Person

Beverly Ann Ozuna-Ulrich was born on January 21, 1951, and disappeared from Belle Fourche, SD, on October 17th, 2003.

Her estranged husband claimed she left home in a vehicle with someone that evening and has never been seen again. Her family reported her missing 10 days later. Although she had taken unscheduled trips before, she'd always let family know where she was going and when she'd be back. She'd been separated from her husband for a year to a year and a half, but their separation was friendly, and she regularly visited his home to spend time with their children and cook and clean.

Beverly is Lakota Indian, approximately 5' tall, 130 pounds, and has graying dark brown/black hair and brown eyes. She has a tattoo "Steven" on her upper arm, and her right eyebrow is pierced.

She was last seen wearing blue bell-bottom jeans and a gray t-shirt.

If you know any details about the disappearance of Beverly Ulrich, please contact
Butte County Sheriff's office at (605) 892-3324 or
DCI Agent Steve Ardis at (605) 391-6661 or
SD DCI at (605) 773=3331

Photo courtesy of Krista Ulrich
(Ref: The Charley Project; Krista Ulrich)

    Anyone who knew Beverly Ulrich-Ozuna knew the everlasting impression she left with them. Beverly was a very happy woman. She had the softest heart anyone could have. She was the light to anyone's day. She always had fun and wanted everyone around her to laugh and have a smile on their face.

    It was a rare occasion to ever see her without a heartwarming smile on her face. Beverly was very passionate about caring for her family, as you would always find her with her children making memories. If she wasn't with her family, she was out with close friends dancing to her favorite music. Always pulling people in to dance and have a good time. She was a great mother to all of her children. Growing up she didn't have the best home life but that made her strive harder to try and make life for her kids better.

    Beverly had five boys and four girls. She was always the number one fan to her kids, as she would do whatever her children wanted if that meant attending all games or watching their favorite sports on TV. As we grew up and became more independent we always knew that when the streetlights came on or we heard that whistle it was her. She was a huge family person and loved her mom unconditionally. This is where we spent some of our time just enjoying time with her and her mother. Beverly was one of 16 children. She grew up learning how to cook clean and take care of her siblings at such a young age.

Losing my mother is a very hard thing mentally and physically. You really don't realize how much they really do teach you in life. Growing up without her was the hardest thing for me as I was very close to her. To this day, I would love to pick up the phone and call her to hear her voice or for life advice. Mothers, do make everything in your life seem okay. I wouldn't wish anyone to go through the hurt and pain my family has endured since she left.

I want anyone who is dealing with the same situation whether it be a mom, sister, or whoever to never give up hope and never stop fighting. Knowing every day I can't or don't understand why this person would ever do such a cruel thing is hard to live with. As I sit and watch my children grow and learn new things in life they don't get to call or have a grandma around to experience these things in life.

If I had the chance to say anything to you, Mom, it is that I'm beyond proud of you and all you went through in your life. You overcame every obstacle that came in your way. You were and are a great mother. We appreciate it all. I promise you, Mom, that I will keep your story alive and I won't ever give up on finding some answers for you. Just please know you are truly missed by a lot of people here. We miss you so much, Mom.

By Krista Ulrich

Carmen Charger and Delmas Traversie, Jr. Unsolved Deaths

Somewhere between March 13, 2019 and March 15, 2019, during a raging snowstorm, Carmen Charger and Delmas Traversie, Jr., were killed at House 717, No Heart Housing, in Eagle Butte, SD.

Carmen, also known as "Happy," was 39 years old and a mother of two children, a son and a daughter.

Delmas, nicknamed "Cactus," was an enrolled member of the Cheyenne River Sioux Tribe Indian Reservation, 63 years old, and the father to three children, a son and two daughters.

Family members state that Carmen had been staying with Delmas for a while.

The FBI is offering a reward of up to $10,000 for information that leads to an arrest and conviction in the Delmas Traversie, Jr. and Carmen Charger homicide case. (Ref: *KELOLAND News*, April 14, 2021)

For your consideration:

~ The cause of death is not listed in any information about this case. Would this information be a key piece of evidence in finding the perpetrators?

~ Is it possible the perpetrator(s) lived nearby, given that a blizzard was going on during the time they were likely killed?

~ What possible motive would anyone have to hurt a young woman and an older man, especially two who were known as loving, gentle, and happy people?

If you know anything about the murders of Carmen Charger and Delmas Traversie, Jr., please contact:

FBI's Minneapolis Field Office at (763) 569-8000
Or the FBI tipline at 1-800-225-5324
Or Online at https://www.fbi.gov.contact-us/field-offices
Or CrimeStoppers at 1-800-222-TIPS.

(Ref: FBI; *KOTA Territory News*; justicefornativewomen.com)

My brother was an excellent guitar player—he could have put Van Halen to shame. He was a big-hearted, caring man. He was a Son, Brother, Uncle, Father, Lala, and a friend.

I pray that he had a good journey to the spirit world. And to whoever did this to my brother, Karma will get you.
Dana Schlecht

*Photo courtesy of Dana Schlecht

Delmas Emmett Traversie, Jr., Wanhinkpe cik 'ala "Little Arrow," was Delmas, Sr. and Elvira's first-born son, welcomed with loving arms and pride. From the day he was born, he was affectionately known as Cactus.

After graduating from Cheyenne Eagle Butte High School, he attended college at the University of South Dakota in Vermillion. While there, he met and married Audrey DeLong and they had two children, Vincent and Nicole.

Delmas later joined the Navy. When he was discharged in 1988, he returned to Eagle Butte where he met his life partner, Delvina Morrison, with whom he shared his life until her death in 2017. Together they had three children, two deceased and one living, Elvira L. Traversie. Delmas enjoyed his family and friends immensely, and was known for his kind and generous heart, willing to help anyone who needed it, especially if it involved working on cars. He was incredibly skilled in automotive mechanics and repair.

We miss our beloved brother, dad, uncle and son, Delmas Traversie, Jr. - Gail (sister)

*Photo courtesy of Gail Traversie

If your loved one's case is not in this book and you would like to see it included in a possible second book, please contact me through my website at www.christinemagerwevik.com

Alicia Marie Folkers Hummel Unsolved Death

It was a warm, sunny day, June 1, 2015, and Alicia Hummel, 29, wanted to go fishing on her first day of a month-long vacation between jobs. She was known for spontaneity and sharing her life with her followers on Facebook and Snapchat.

"I'm going fishing!" her post on Facebook stated, as she headed for a rural Vermillion, SD, fishing spot called Myron Grove. She shared her plans for the day on Snapchat, posting a picture of her fishing pole sticking out the open sunroof of her car.

Alicia, a preschool teacher, was separated from her husband and living in Sioux City with her grandparents, Duane and Jan Folkers.

That sunny Monday afternoon on June 1st, Alicia posted shortly before 1:00 p.m. saying she was "starting over" because she'd misplaced her tackle box. At 1:06 p.m., she purchased a fishing license at the Vermillion Walmart. Shortly afterward, at 1:19 p.m., she sent a text to a friend, stating that an old man who'd sold her the license had said he hoped she "caught a big one."

At 1:30 p.m., Alicia posted on Snapchat, "Finally I've been waiting since fall," showing a picture of Myron Grove boat dock. Just after she arrived at the dock, at 1:45 p.m., she texted a friend, saying, "Apparently, it's a nice day to get it on in the car midday too lmao."

A short time later, between 2 and 3:30 p.m. (varying times, according to separate sources), a Game, Fish, and Parks employee found Alicia's body in the water next to the dock. In one article in Fargo's InForum, Clay County,

SD, Sheriff Andy Howe says, "We believe that we have a very narrow time frame between her arriving in the area, her being killed, and her being discovered...a very narrow time frame."

Autopsy reports list Alicia's cause of death as drowning, but she had also sustained a large laceration to her neck, and blunt force trauma to the head. Her manner of death is listed as homicide.

Authorities would later state that the initial attack had started about 10-15 feet from the water where she was found, and that they did not believe that the neck wound was the "byproduct of the struggle," but was intended as a means to cause harm. They would not comment about whether she'd been sexually assaulted. Toxicology reports state that there were no signs of alcohol or other substances found in her system.

Alicia's car keys were found on the front seat of her car, which was parked in the lot nearby. Years after Alicia's murder, authorities also revealed that they had found Alicia's cell phone, but would not elaborate on where it was found or what, if any, evidence they found on it. They would not comment on whether the fishing pole was found. A year after her murder, college students found her purse on a dry sandbar on the river with all the contents intact.

Alicia's husband, Tony, was eliminated as a suspect, as he was over 200 miles away in Pierre, SD, with relatives.

The Game, Fish, and Parks employee was questioned multiple times and was able to provide a description of a loud, dark-colored sedan with tinted windows, but it hasn't led to any suspects. Sheriff Howe expressed his frustration that, though this is a popular area that sees a lot of fishermen and boaters, and it was a perfect, sunny day, not one person has come forward to state they were present or even in the general vicinity.

In an interview that Jan Folkers gave to *KELOLAND News*'s Angela Kennecke, she states that one investigator mentioned that they'd found a pair of men's shoes at the site, resembling ones that a man "would wear in a restaurant." It appeared as if someone had taken them off to avoid getting them wet in the water.

Myron Grove has one road leading into it; one that branches off to the dock where she was found, and the other leading to private residences, but it's a popular public area that anyone can get to.

There are few and dwindling leads in this case, despite multiple agencies' involvement, but Sheriff Howe is confident they will be able to solve the case. He states in one interview that they have, and continue to attain, cell phone records for "digital avenues" to solving Alicia's murder. Sheriff Howe says, "We do have suspects, but we don't have a case."

For your consideration:
~ Did Alicia see something or someone she was not supposed to and was killed for it?
~ Might cell phone records for area towers be able to reveal who was in the area around the time of Alicia's death?
~ Is there DNA evidence that might connect her to a suspect?
~ How is it possible that such a popular spot, in the middle of such a perfect day, did not have any traffic or visitors? Why is *no one* who may have been in the vicinity coming forward?

~ Do the men's shoes found at the scene belong to the perpetrator? Was there DNA obtained from those shoes?

A $5000 reward is being offered for anyone with information leading to an arrest in Alicia's murder.

If you know anything about the murder of Alicia Hummel, please contact
Clay County Sheriff's Office at (605) 677-7100
Or submit an anonymous tip to claysheriff.org.

(Ref: *InForum*; *KELOLAND News*; *NBC News*; *KTIV*; *KCAU-TV*; Jan Folkers)

Alicia was our first grandchild. She and her mom were living with us so we got very attached to her. It was so much fun watching her grow up. One of her aunts owned a dance studio so when Alicia was old enough, we put her in dance classes until high school. She was also in band in Jr and Sr High.

When she went off to college in Brookings (SDSU), she tried out for flags and performed with them the next four years.

Alicia was always including me in shopping trips, movies, and even a concert. She always made sure we came to watch her perform at the football games. She was always ready to help someone else.

On the morning of her death, we had breakfast together and were discussing plans for the day. She was going to find a girlfriend to go fishing with her. She said to me, "Grandma, you should go with me." But her grandpa had surgery and I felt I needed to stay home. I told her not to go alone. I still carry the guilt for not being there to protect her.

I just wish one person would come forward to say who did this. We lost a very loving young woman. Love you, Alicia.

Jan Folkers, grandmother

*Photo courtesy of Jan Folkers

What words do you use to describe Alicia? Those words are plentiful because she was everything to everyone she met.

I first met Alicia when she applied to work for me when I owned my daycare. She fit. She loved kids. She loved her co-workers. She gave her all to every child and adult she met. My staff, the kids, and their parents were all family.

Alicia remained close by my side through some of my darkest days. She was my beacon. I never strayed far from her light. She was my peace, my comfort, my strength when my world collapsed. She never second-guessed her place in my life...I never second-guessed her place in mine. I only wish distance hadn't gotten in the way when she was struggling.. she knew I loved her, I knew she loved me.

I will never forget my heartbreak when I learned someone had taken her from us. I asked God "why?". I soon had the answer. She gave her all for us, so God rewarded her with Heaven.

Her memories fill my life. Stories of her are plentiful... and funny! We had gone fishing at the same location of her death. I caught a massive catfish...she caught its offspring! She posed for several pictures with this fish. Fishing was her peace. She loved Myron Grove. She loved the beauty that surrounded her. I hope she was at peace at the time of her passing. I know she fought with vigor, but when God called, I hope she found herself at peace.

I know her friends and family struggle daily with her passing. We should look to Heaven and be peace-filled knowing she is with God. Why? Because Alicia loved God. She had God first in her life, that was the way she was raised. A child of God. Alicia›s short life was filled with love. She was love and we can never forget that love we have for her and she STILL has for us!

Margo Logue, friend

Morgan Aryn Bauer
South Dakota Ties
Missing Person

On February 12, 2016, Morgan Bauer, a native of Aberdeen, SD, arrived in Atlanta, GA, from Minneapolis, MN. She'd made arrangements with a man she'd met on Craigslist to stay at his home and perform household duties in exchange for room and board. She did not have a job lined up ahead of time, other than this. She'd borrowed $20 from a friend before leaving for Atlanta and was waiting for a tax return to be loaded onto her H&R Block Card in her name.

On her second day in Atlanta, her living arrangement fell through, and she was kicked out of the home. She found a room at a local hotel, and desperate for work, she took a job at a former strip club called Top of Gainesville in Gainesville, Georgia.

She then returned to Atlanta and had posted on Facebook on February 25th stating she'd gotten a job at another strip club called Tease Gentlemen's Club on Cheshire Bridge Road in Atlanta. Her post said, "And I work here." (That post has since mysteriously disappeared with no explanation from Facebook.)

All social media contact and phone contact by Morgan with her friends stopped after this date. A friend of Morgan's in South Dakota contacted Sherri Keenan, Morgan's mother, when she hadn't heard from Morgan in days, which was completely out of character for her. Sherri and Morgan had had a disagreement shortly before Morgan left, and Sherri attributed her lack of communication to their disagreement. Sherri flew to Atlanta to start the search for her daughter.

Sherri arrived in Atlanta on March 14th and immediately began contacting any persons or businesses that may have had contact with Morgan. Sherri spoke with the owner of Top of Gainesville where Morgan worked, and the owner told Sherri that Morgan worked there from February 19-25th. He told Sherri that Morgan was scheduled to work on the 26th but did not show up, and was never heard from afterward. Sherri knew from Morgan's Facebook post that Morgan was last seen at Tease, auditioning for the job, and learned that Morgan did not have the legal permit to work there, and therefore wasn't hired (despite Morgan's Facebook claim that she worked there.) Morgan had auditioned at Tease with a Top coworker, Katelyn.

There are conflicting reports from various club workers about Morgan leaving in different vehicles around the time of her disappearance, but the only consistent story Sherri continued to hear was that Morgan had auditioned at Tease and was last seen leaving with a girl named Katelyn and Katelyn's boyfriend, Alex.

Sherri spoke with a manager at Tease and asked about the last time Morgan had been seen there on the 25th, and he confirmed this detail. He later called Sherri back to inform her that Katelyn, the girl who Morgan was last seen with, was in the club at that very moment. Sherri instructed him to put Katelyn on the phone with her, which he did. Sherri and Katelyn spoke on the phone until Sherri, and two women who were assisting her, arrived at the club and spoke with her and her boyfriend in person.

Katelyn told Sherri that she and her boyfriend didn't know where Morgan was, but that they knew of a friend of Morgan's named Plug, who might have spoken with Morgan before she went missing. They supplied his phone number and Sherri spoke with him, and even saw the last texts that Plug and Morgan had exchanged. Plug and Morgan had texted off and on in the days before her disappearance, and on the night of the 25th, just after midnight (thereby, the 26th), Morgan had texted him saying she hadn't made much money that night and needed more. He texted her the next morning and three other times that day with no response.

When Sherri was speaking with Katelyn and Alex that day, they repeatedly stated that they hadn't seen her, but later changed their stories and admitted that they had left Tease with Morgan on the night of February 25th and later gave her a ride to a CITGO station in Covington, GA. They claim they saw Morgan get into a green Mitsubishi Eclipse with someone. Their story is unverified, however, as there was no surveillance to support their claim.

Sherri later acquired evidence that Morgan's phone last pinged just after midnight on the 26th (possibly after her last text with Plug) near Porterdale, GA, where Katelyn and Alex lived with his father. Police did not initially question Katelyn and Alex until Sherri involved other authorities. They did do a cursory search of an area behind the premises where Katelyn and Alex lived, but found nothing. Much later, police questioned Katelyn and Alex, searched their property, and brought in search dogs to pick up a scent, but it had been too long and the dog search did not garner any results.

Sherri hired a private investigator, hung and handed out thousands of fliers, spoke with news outlets, reached out to missing persons organizations, and purchased billboard space with information about her missing daughter in her attempts to locate her.

Morgan was 19 when she went missing, is 5'6" tall and weighs approximately 130 pounds. She has brown hair and green eyes. Her ears are gauged, she has two lip piercings, and a pierced navel. She has several tattoos: a sun and moon inside a Celtic four-star design near her right shoulder on her chest; an anchor with a sentence, "Whatever you love can be taken away, so live like it's your dying day" on her inner left wrist; on her left hip, "It's in herself she will find the strength she needs;" on the back of her neck, a black tree of life with tiny flowers; a blue and orange jellyfish on the inside of her right forearm.

There is currently a $10,000 reward being offered for information regarding Morgan's whereabouts.

For your consideration:

~ Could Morgan be a victim of human trafficking? If so, what can be done to find her? Are law enforcement officials doing everything they can to pursue those leads?

~ Does the couple who first denied seeing Morgan on the night of February 27th have something to do with her disappearance? Why would they deny it and then admit to dropping her off at CITGO?

~ Despite the disagreement between Sherri and Morgan, why and how would Morgan, who was close to her family and friends, suddenly and completely stop all contact with them, even through birthdays, holidays, and special events?

~ Morgan was a gregarious, social creature, constantly posting on multiple forms of social media. Would that have suddenly stopped, even if she wanted to cut herself loose from all family and friend connections?

~ Morgan is still listed as a missing person in Atlanta, GA. Do law enforcement officials plan to pursue the obvious leads to the ex-coworker and her boyfriend?

If you know anything about the disappearance of Morgan Aryn Bauer, please contact

Atlanta Police Department at (404) 546-4235

Or to submit an anonymous tip, contact Atlanta CrimeStoppers at (404) 577-8477

Or this toll free tip line set up by Keenana at 1-(855) 667-4262.

Photo courtesy of Sherri Keenan

(Ref: *Aberdeen American News*; Stories of the Unsolved; Sherri Keenan)

Dear Morgan,

My darling daughter, it has taken me so long to write this that I stopped counting the days. I was asked to write a letter regarding what I would say to you if I could say anything right now...

I'm sorry. I would tell you how sorry I am if I ever made you feel small or not courageous enough. I'm sorry if I made you feel ashamed and not brave. I'm sorry if I didn't see the whole of you because I only saw the child. I am sorry if I created a space where being treated with anything other than love and respect seemed like an option. I am sorry if I didn't teach you you're worth and how to value your whole self. I'm sorry if any of my actions have brought you to this place - where ever you may be.

Know my love, wherever that place is, I am with you. You are loved, you are wanted and you are needed. I am grateful for you. You have always been my heart. I want to hold your hand, I want to see your smile, I want to hear you laugh. I want to brush your hair. I want to help you choose your wedding dress and hold your children. I want you to be safe and happy. I want to see your face at Christmas and the wrinkles that form there as you grow older. I want to hear all of your secrets and watch bad movies while doing laundry. I want to tell you I love you every day. I want you to come home. Please bring Morgan home. I love you. I'm sorry. Please forgive me. Thank you.

All my love,
Mom

Morgan...

This is by far the hardest letter I'll ever write and if it was on paper it would already be bathing in tears. Where to begin with endless things to say. You can brighten a day more than any sun in the sky. You can turn any frown upside down with just your own smile. Your bubbly personality is infectious and can make everything better. From your run and jump hugs to your sweet and kind generosity. You're the essence of joy and the epitome of positivity. My life hasn't been the same without you, nor can it or will it ever. There really aren't words for how much this world, my world, can get any better without you. The slightest thought of you, which is constant, sends my emotions reeling just to talk to you again, see you again, to just know that you're okay!

My life is crumbling in so many ways and I NEED YOU! I miss you so much it kills me. You will ALWAYS be in my heart, my mind and deep in my soul.

I love you Always and Forever and beyond.
Aunt Kya
P.S. please come back in my life...

Hello Morgan

Where are you? I miss you so much.

I think about you everyday. Going through pictures reminds me of you. I remember so many things...

When you were 1 or 2, your car pulled in on the driveway. I was so excited to see your mom. It was so long since we saw each other. I couldn't wait to meet you. Then your mom handed you to me. You were a beautiful little one. So precious.

We had fun when you were on the farm with me. It was a fun day when we went out to the pasture to see Princess. She was a bottle calf when she was a baby, the next year, she had her own baby. You wanted to ride her, but I said "No, she would probably buck you off".

You had fun on the tractor rides, climbing on the hay, and playing with the cats.

When I moved to town, you would twirl around and around on the clothesline pole. You would giggle. It was so fun to hear your happy and giggly laugh. One of your favorite things was jumping on a friends trampoline. You liked watching and petting her big horses too.

A few years later, Lester and I were living in the Black Hills. You, grandma Pfeiffer, Paige and Gavin came to see us. You were able to see deer, chipmunks and other wild animals that came into our yard and almost up on our deck. We went to Crazy Horse too. There we ate, looked at Crazy Horse mountain, looked through the telescopes and took photographs. We rode the 4 wheeler too. A couple of days later, on your way back to Aberdeen, grandma Pfeiffer took you, Paige and Gavin to Reptile Gardens. It sure was a fun visit and the time went so fast.

A couple of years later, when Lester and I moved back to Aberdeen, I was doing a lot of doctoring, as I had developed numerous health issues.

One day, you came to visit by yourself. I was having a feel-lousy day. You said "grandma, why do we have to sit here? Why can't you do anything with me?" I tried to explain that I was trying out new medications, because I had such shortness of breath, so I couldn't be real active. We settled on a few games of Crazy 8s and coloring. I felt terrible, what could I do? On this day, I felt like there was a change in our relationship. I wasn't a fun grandma anymore. I'm so sorry.

Less than a year later, Lester and I moved back to Chamberlain, SD, where he was offered a job back in law enforcement.

We hardly saw anyone anymore. It seemed that everyone was so busy with their families and other things. That's as it should be. I tried to get back to see you all monthly or whenever I could get there. It didn't always happen though, because I worked too.

It was so much fun when we would have pool parties for birthdays and other things. As time went, I struggled with my breathing, so I couldn't go to the parties anymore. It was so fun to see the photos and videos that others sent to me. I treasure them so much. There is one where you were hanging on the side of the pool with the cutest smile. You were having so much fun.

I miss you Morgan, where are you?

Do you remember your high school graduation reception? It was fun making the tie dye cupcakes. You gave me the biggest hug.

The holidays have always meant get togethers. Especially at Christmas. Almost everyone came for grandma Pfeiffer, and to see the rest of us too. A person never knew if there was someone extra coming. It touched my heart so much, to see the interactions between each and every one of you. Once at the place for the Christmas celebration, animated conversations and playful arguing would happen. I could always hear your happy and playful voice. It could often be heard over all of the other voices.

Morgan, you loved grandma Pfeiffer and always had such a great relationship with her and it showed. I'm not sure if you know that grandma passed away three years ago..

I want to thank you for the pictures that you sent to me.

Christmas of 2015 was especially fun. We got together at Brandi's house. It seemed that more photos were taken and more interactions. I don't think that I smiled so much or hugged as much. You are in so many pictures. I wish that I could share them with you. I will, as soon as I know where to send them.

Then came 2016.

The new year began without a hitch. I would guess it began with me writing for Health Union or moderating their COPD site. I also could have been checking sites that I have. I don't know if my hubby worked that day. Maybe, we did nothing. I know that it was uneventful. 2016, another year. My how time flies.

I know for sure that I checked the Missing Morgan #missingmorgan site.

March 11, was my birthday. I often say that if something is going to happen, it will happen on my birthday.

On March 11, 2016, that's the date that our world stayed still.

It was on that day that I found out that you were missing. No one has seen you since February 25, 2016. We know that you caught a ride to Minneapolis MN, then you flew from there to Atlanta, GA. We know you took a cleaning job for *one night and then had to go. It was as if you dropped from the face of the earth. Your mom talked to people from the area. She flew from Aberdeen to Atlanta to try to find you. She wanted to be sure that you were okay.*

I have to admit, I was so overwhelmed and terrified. I was having trouble understanding what your mom had told me and what she shared after. I don't think that I did everything I was supposed to do. I did the report to NamUs, which was filed with them on March 15, 2016.

Your mom had a person, Kasey McClure that she met in the Atlanta area, and another who knew the area and the clubs in the area, as well as other dancers. I've talked with her a few times over the years. She's amazing, she really cares.

Someone else told me to contact Cynthia Caron with Lost'n Missing. She is a wonderful person that helps find the missing. Best of all, I could talk to her and share my fears. That means so much.

I've also tried reaching out to other families with a missing person. Some of them reach out to help families as well.

I could never imagine that we would lose you. You were always a family person, especially with grandma. Holidays and birthdays were always so important. It hasn't been the same without you. I sure hope that we hear from you soon. If not to come home, just to let us know that you are okay. I'm terrified and lost. I pray that you aren't suffering.

My mind goes back to the happy days and to the days that you weren't always happy with me. I pray for the day when I can hold you. When it's time we can talk, hopefully we won't be in a hurry.

After this, Morgan, I am so grateful for your tattoos and ear gauges. Those will identify you, as well as other missing persons.

I want others to know that the police department will often do fingerprints. My adult kids were fingerprinted by a visit to safety town when they were kindergarten + ages. It's so important to have records and up to date pictures. Take some regular ones and those with different hairdos and color changes. Keep track of the dentist who has the families dental records. Be safe.

Thank you for praying for my beautiful granddaughter and never stop.

Janet Pfeiffer Plank

Cody White Pipe
Unsolved Death

On September 9th, 2014, on a lonely stretch of highway about five miles east of Vetal, SD, lay Cody White Pipe, 21 years old, and the victim of a brutal hit and run. After the unknown vehicle struck him, he waved his red bandana to flag down a passing vehicle.

The passing drivers, three women, found him lying near the road on US Highway 18, about 5 a.m. and called 911. Two of the women went to get help, and one woman, Jessica, stayed with him until an ambulance arrived. He was taken by ambulance to Bennett County Hospital, about 20 miles from the accident site, where he later died from his injuries.

Jo Denoyer, Cody's sister, says that Cody had been to her house the evening before and had told her that he wanted to go to his friend's wake in Evergreen. He'd been sitting on her porch during the night, and she'd checked on him multiple times. Around 3 a.m., she checked on him, and he was gone. He'd left to hitch a ride or walk to Evergreen. At 9:30 a.m., Jo received a message to contact the police because Cody had been in an accident in Martin. According to Jo, on the way to the accident sight, the ambulance got lost, losing valuable time. She states that although Cody was in bad shape, Jessica, one of the women who had found him, held his hand while they waited, and he told her how pretty she was.

Members of Cody's family believe the driver of the unknown vehicle made no attempt to avoid hitting Cody, or perhaps even went out of their way to hit him. When the family went to the spot where he was found to erect a cross in his memory, they discovered vehicle tracks, still visible in the ditch on both sides of the road. Given Cody's distance from the road when he was found, it seemed apparent that he was struck by a vehicle traveling at a high rate of speed.

September 9th, while Cody walked along the highway, was during a super moon phase, and the nighttime hours were bright and well lit. It would not have been difficult to see what—or who—was walking along the side of the road.

Investigators don't know how much time had passed between the hit and run and when he was found.

For your consideration:
~ Why would someone go out of their way to hit an innocent man walking along the road? Why not just report it as an accident?
~ Was the driver of the unknown vehicle drunk or otherwise under the influence?
~ Cody was alive and cognizant enough to flag down a passing car. Could he have uttered any words to the good Samaritan or the EMTs?
~ Why were there tracks on both sides of the road? Does it indicate that the driver stopped to see what he or she had hit, and turned around?

If you know anything about the driver or the vehicle that was involved in this hit and run, please contact the South Dakota DCI at (605) 394-2258

Or submit an anonymous tip through the DCI tip line at (605) 394-1884.

(Ref: *Lakota Country Times; Rapid City Journal*; Jo Denoyer)

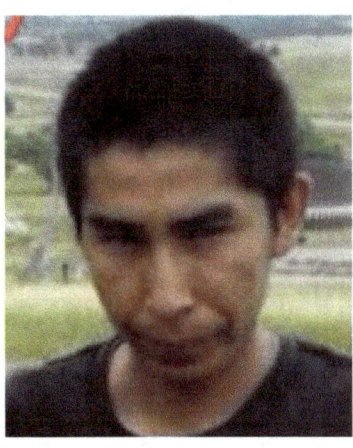

My baby brother, Cody James White Pipe, was born one of a kind. He grew up fast. He learned a lot at a young age, growing up on Pine Ridge and Rosebud Reservations in his short life.

One of my best memories is teaching Cody how to ride a bike. He was only 3 years old when he figured out how to ride a bike. After that, Cody always had wheels to get him where he was going. He could never be in one spot for too long.

Cody used to love going from one sister's house to another sister's house to stay, and enjoyed being with family. All his nieces and nephews loved when their Uncle Cody came to stay. He taught them how to fix their bikes.

Cody always found a way to work to earn money to provide for himself. He worked on cars and trucks. That's what he loved doing. It didn't matter whose car Cody was driving, he always made sure he smoked the wheels.

How could anyone run over another human being and leave them there like that? Remembering my brother is painful, but I don't want to forget him, either. I want to see justice for him.

Aimee White Pipe

*Photo courtesy of Jessica Nicole Ritz)

My brother, Cody, was a wanderer and a hippie. We nicknamed him Petey. He would always pop in—he seemed to know exactly when he was needed. He wandered in and out of everyone's lives, but everywhere he went, he left a piece of himself.

After the passing of our father, he felt the need to fill his shoes—to be our caretakers, our rescuer. If someone was having car trouble, he was right there. He'd pop in and work on the house if something needed fixing. If we needed a babysitter, he was right there. He was very family oriented. He loved kids, especially his nieces and nephews, and his nieces and nephews flocked to him, but he never wanted kids for himself. He liked to be there for the sisters.

Cody was a jack of all trades. He knew how to do it all, and did whatever work he could find to make money for himself. He'd somehow know exactly when to show up for family get-togethers, birthdays, Christmas, he always knew exactly when to pop in.

He loved the elders and they loved him. Many have said he had the heart of an old soul. But Cody had an awesome, sarcastic and somewhat dark sense of humor. He always knew how to make us laugh, even when we shouldn't.

I always remember Petey saying, "Why are you crying (over one fish)? You're in the ocean!" He always knew how to put us back together.

The pain never goes away. They took our heart. We never stop asking why, or going through the what if's or how come's, we plead with God for answers or to take it back. We never stop saying we're sorry for not protecting him. They say time heals, but I don't agree. Time is slowly killing us. We miss our brother.

When that person hit him, they took away our family glue. He held the family together, like our father had before he died. Our hearts are raw. We try to move past his death, but we can't. We can hardly talk about it. But when his favorite song, Johnny Cash's "Hurt" comes on, we turn it up. We know he's watching over us.

"All we got is us," he used to say. I can remember him drilling this into our minds. And now that he's gone, we feel incomplete. We're not us anymore. Yet we feel as if any moment, he's going to pop in.

Jo Denoyer

Dana Mae Adamson
Unsolved Death

On an early spring Sunday morning in Centerville, SD, March 24, 2002, Rayne Adamson called authorities, telling them his wife, Dana Mae Adamson, was dead of a suspected suicide.

Shortly after turning 18, Dana Levasseur had married Rayne Adamson after only dating him for two weeks. He had recently resigned his position as Centerville's Chief of Police to run the family bar, The Desert Inn. Things went well for Dana and Rayne, at first. But within mere months of her short marriage to Rayne, her sisters began to notice signs that things were not going well between the newlyweds. Two nights before Dana was found dead, Breann, Dana's older sister, noticed bruises on Dana's neck and rug burns on her forehead. Dana told her she and Rayne had gotten into a fight after the bar had closed.

Witnesses told authorities that the night before Dana was found dead, Dana and Rayne had been at a party, and that Dana had left first, and Rayne left later. She was found dead the next morning on her living room couch.

Dana's sisters claim that rather than calling 911 from their home, Rayne ran to a neighbor's and asked them to call authorities, for some reason, and that when law enforcement arrived, Rayne's dad and aunt (who was with first responders), were already on the scene.

When authorities arrived, they immediately taped off the residence to preserve the scene, and began an investigation into Dana's death.

Now-retired DCI Detective Jim Severson was called in as a special agent to investigate Dana's death. He and now-retired Sheriff Byron Nogelmeier worked together to investigate the case, questioning Rayne for over 8 hours. Dana's sister, Jen Boeyink, stated that she had heard that Rayne's account of what happened changed several times. Detective Severson stated in an interview on *KELOLAND News*, when asked what happened after they arrived home, "Well, that depends on whether or not you believe what he says, or you believe what the crime scene tells you. Two different stories that contradict each other. The crime scene does not match the 8-8 ½ hours we interviewed him."

Byron Nogelmeier stated in his *KELO* interview, "Could this be a suicide? Possible. Could it be a murder? Probable. Could this be an assisted suicide? Possible." He stated in this interview that the trajectory of the bullet entered the back of the head, out the front of the head, and it didn't seem that would be a way to commit suicide.

According to Dana's sister, Jen Boeyink, Dana was making plans to leave Rayne a couple months before her death and had slowly begun removing personal belongings from the home discreetly so he wouldn't suspect she was leaving. At one point during the marriage of Dana and Rayne, Jen had invited Dana to bring Rayne over for supper so Jen could get to know him, but Dana declined the invitation because she didn't want Rayne to know where Jen lived, in case Dana needed to run. Jen states that this is the first sense she had of how serious (wrong) things were between Dana and Rayne.

Jen also states that a few weeks before Dana's death, things were growing tenser between Dana and Rayne, and Jen told Dana she should hide the guns because Jen was worried for her sister. Dana said she didn't think he'd ever use them on her.

When Breann, Dana's other sister, asked Rayne what happened, he stated that he was in the bedroom, Dana was in the living room, and he heard a pop, and it sounded like she'd "shot the water heater." Dana's family states that she was in great spirits and would never have committed suicide.

During questioning, Rayne agreed to a lie detector test and failed. Although there is enough suspicion to point toward Rayne, lie detector tests are not admissible in court, they are not completely dependable, nor are they proof of guilt. Law enforcement officials do not have enough evidence to pursue or guarantee a conviction.

Authorities told *KELOLAND News* reporter, Angela Kennecke, that a key piece of evidence is missing: the top she'd been wearing, a butterfly halter-top had disappeared. They stated that if they could find a witness that could come forward to tell them they saw Dana at her home, wearing this top while Rayne was present, that it could be a huge step in moving forward in Dana's case. They suspect that she had changed clothes, there had been a struggle, and at some point afterward, a gun ended her life.

In an unrelated case, three years after Dana's death, Rayne was arrested and charged with sexual contact and rape of a 14-year-old girl. The contact and rape charges were later dropped, but he was then charged and convicted of two counts of witness tampering and providing alcohol to a minor. He was sentenced to eight years in prison, which he tried to get overturned and failed. Shortly after he was released, the victim placed a protection order against Rayne, but it was dropped when the victim failed to appear in court. Another protection order was placed against him and later dropped as well.

For your consideration:
~ There are no public reports as to whether gun shot residue was found on either Dana or Rayne. Do authorities know the answer to this and hold this info close to the vest?
~ Why would Rayne run to the neighbors to have them call authorities rather than call from his own home? Did Rayne question them about what they may have heard while he was there? Was he trying to get his alibi straight?
~ Did or does Rayne's conviction point to a propensity for grooming or violence against young females, and was Dana one of his victims?
~ Where is the butterfly halter-top? Was there evidence on that article of clothing that pointed toward the perpetrator?

If you know anything about the death of Dana Adamson or any of the circumstances surrounding the events leading up to her death or the missing halter-top, please contact:

Turner County Sheriff at (605) 297-3225
Centerville Police Department at (605) 563-3911
SD DCI at (605) 773-3331
Or DCI tip line at (605) 394-1884 to leave an anonymous tip.

Photos courtesy of Breann Meyer and Jen Boeyink
(Ref: *KELOLAND News; Argus Leader*; Breann Meyer; Jen Boeyink)

Dana,

I have a picture of you on my desk. I look at it every day, and when I do, it's so easy to forget that you're not with us anymore, and that you haven't been for twenty years now. The picture looks so fresh and new, as though it was just taken last week, rather than the year you turned seventeen. You were just stepping into the woman you were meant to become, and despite bumps in your own road, you were always trying to show those you loved how much they meant to you. I still remember my favorite birthday, when you showed up unannounced, surprised me with pizza and a dolphin figurine, and spent the night just hanging out and watching movies. That meant more to me than you could have ever known, but then you were always trying to make other people happy—it was one of your gifts. It makes me wonder what kind of a woman you'd be, and how our family would be different if your death hadn't changed us irrevocably forever. I miss you, every day, and I miss who we would have all been if you hadn't been taken from us. My peace now comes from knowing that mom is with you and you aren't alone anymore. I love you forever, ~Sissy.

From Jen Boeyink

Dana was a warm and loving person who enjoyed talking and laughing with family and friends. Dana was a very trusting person and made friends easily, always ready for an adventure and not afraid to try new things, very get up and go if you will. Dana couldn't wait to see what the future would bring, that became especially true when she became an aunt for the first time, she absolutely adored her niece. She often told me she couldn't wait to have her own kids someday. Dana had such a sweet and uplifting personality, she loved to joke and laugh. Her laugh was contagious; anyone within a few feet of hearing her laughing started laughing too. I'll never forget that laugh. Dana had a fire for life that I would have never imagined to have extinguished at only 18 years old, without living out any of the dreams she used to talk to me about. I sure wish we knew what happened that morning so we could have some closure. If I could tell her anything right now it would be that I have missed her every single day since the day she had to leave us and that I haven't let her memory die, all of her nieces and nephew know all about her and we all love her so much. Her life mattered, I didn't just lose my sister, she was a daughter, granddaughter, aunt and a friend. The list could go on but because her life was short we all missed out on so many things. I miss her, WE miss her and HER LIFE MATTERED.

Breann Meyer (Levasseur)
Dana's sister

Stanley Harris
Missing Person

Stanley Walker Harris, also known as James Fisher or Harris Walker, was last seen in Sioux Falls, SD, on September 20, 2010.

He is Caucasian, 5'5" and approximately 120 pounds, with gray/partially gray hair and blue eyes. His nickname is Stan. He is a transient and has no known medical conditions, though he does use a cane. Stanley has several tattoos: on his left arm is a serpent, eagle, and a knife on his right arm is a tattoo of a bug; and on his abdomen is a tattoo that says, "Don't cry baby."

Stanley's van, which he lived in, was found abandoned in Falls Park, Sioux Falls, SD.

A photo of Stanley Harris can be seen on the SD Attorney General's website.

If you know anything about Stanley's disappearance or his current whereabouts, please contact:
Sioux Falls Police Department at (605) 367-7212
Or to offer an anonymous tip, call CrimeStoppers at (877) 367-7007.

(Ref: Websleuths; The Charley Project)

Startling Statistics

According to the November 2021 publication of the CDC, homicide is the leading cause of death among Native Americans and Alaska Natives, many of them attributed to violence by an intimate partner.

In an article published by the Bureau of Indian Affairs, citing the CDC data, the murder rate is 10 times higher than the national average for women living on the reservations, the third leading cause of death for Native women. They went on to say, "Additionally, this group were significantly more likely to experience a rape in their lifetimes compared to other women. . . More than four in five American Indian and Alaska Native men (86.1%) have experienced violence in their lifetime."

The New York Times stated in a 2012 article that violent crimes on the nation's 310 reservations are more than two and a half times higher than the national average, and that the Justice Department, responsible for prosecuting the more serious crimes on reservations, files charges on only half of murder cases and about a third of sexual assault cases. They state that Native women are raped at more than four times the national average.

They go on to say that Native Americans are frustrated with the low rate of prosecution by the FBI, and that they're treated with a "second-class system of justice, but prosecutors claim that they turn down most because of a lack of admissible evidence." The article quotes, "Under federal law, tribal courts have the authority to prosecute tribal members for crimes committed on reservations but cannot sentence those convicted to more than three years in prison. As a result, tribes usually seek federal prosecution for serious crimes."

Additionally, the NYT article states that tribes feel as though the FBI is not only declining to prosecute but that the tribes are not given reasons or notifications for the declinations, and sometimes, federal prosecutors fail to inform tribes that they've declined a case until after the tribe's statute of limitations has run out. And once the federal government does decline a case, they seldom hand over evidence to the tribal courts.

In a more alarming statement made by the NYT, "The government did not pursue rape charges on reservations 65 percent of the time (last year) and rejected 61 percent of cases involving charges of sexual abuse of children, the federal data showed."

There is very little current data available that shows the disparity in crime rates, solve/clearance rates, and media attention regarding white Americans versus Native American and Alaska Native cases.

To be sure, there are major issues regarding prosecutorial authority between local, tribal, state, and federal jurisdictions. The impact of that lack of cooperation and understanding falls primarily on the Native community and their very lives.

(Ref: CDC.gov; *New York Times;* *KELOLAND News;* Bureau of Justice Statistics)

Alize Millard
Unsolved Death

Alize Millard, a sweet-faced boy of 15, had just graduated 8th grade, ready to start school as a freshman. Within a couple short months, he was found dead. Hikers in the Grass Mountain area of the Rosebud Indian Reservation found Alize hanging from a tree on July 10, 2019.

Initially, law enforcement believed Alize died from suicide, though Alize's family immediately discounted this notion. Then law enforcement officials began to see clues that led them to see his death as suspicious.

Alize lived in the Gregory, SD, area but was spending the summer with his grandparents on the reservation. He'd only been with them for a week when he disappeared one night and was later found dead in a remote and secluded part of the reservation, Ghost Hawk Canyon, also known as Boy Scout Cabin Falls. The area is a known hangout for parties and bonfires.

KELOLAND News interviewed local law enforcement shortly after Alize's death, and law enforcement officials stated that they knew of physical circumstances that they couldn't talk about. In a later interview, they revealed that Alize had died from hanging and was then set on fire. Alize had 3rd and 4th degree burns on his body.

The investigation into Alize's death is ongoing, so the family has not been given or shown a copy of the autopsy report. The medical certificate lists his cause of death as asphyxia, "ligature strangulation, hanging." And the manner of death is as yet, "pending investigation."

Family members, as well as law enforcement officials, suspect there may have been a party happening nearby at the time of his death. Peter Gibbs, Alize's grandfather, stated in the *KELO* interview, "We know of at least 7 people that were there; that were right there when it happened." He also stated that this area is known by teenagers as "the dumping grounds," for reasons other than the liquor bottles and cans found there.

Mr. Gibbs and other family members saved text messages and social media posts boasting about Alize's death and turned them over to investigators. Investigators also collected physical evidence from the area where Alize was found. DNA, if found, may tie suspects to the crime. Family members also believe Alize may have been killed elsewhere and taken to Ghost Hawk Canyon afterward.

Alize's girlfriend believes that his death may be related to local gangs, as Alize knew some of the members, though there is no evidence he was ever involved with local gangs.

Alize's family hasn't received any answers from any law enforcement officials, and though the case is not closed, there seems to be no progress that they know of. Rosebud Sioux Tribal Police admit that the case belongs to the FBI, but the FBI isn't sharing any information with family, if they even have it. Rosebud Sioux Tribal Police state that the FBI has conducted hundreds of interviews, but as yet, this crime is unsolved.

A red flag, a part of Lakota culture, hangs from the tree where Alize's body was found, signifying the place as spiritual and sacred. The red cloth tie can also represent a person asking for prayer, remembrance, or healing.

For your consideration:
~ Is there DNA evidence linking Alize with possible suspects from the area where he was found?

~ Is there evidence that he was killed elsewhere and moved, or hung on the tree, after his death?

~ With texts, social media posts, etc, showing that kids nearby had early knowledge of Alize's death, why is there not more progress in this case?

~ Is Alize's death related to gang violence?

~ What's being done to confront the growing gang-related crimes on reservations?

If you know anything about Alize Millard's death, please contact
Rosebud Sioux Tribal Police at (605) 747-2266
Or the FBI at (605) 224-1331
Or to submit an anonymous tip, contact the FBI at tips.fbi.gov

(Ref: *KELOLAND News*, Jamie Millard)

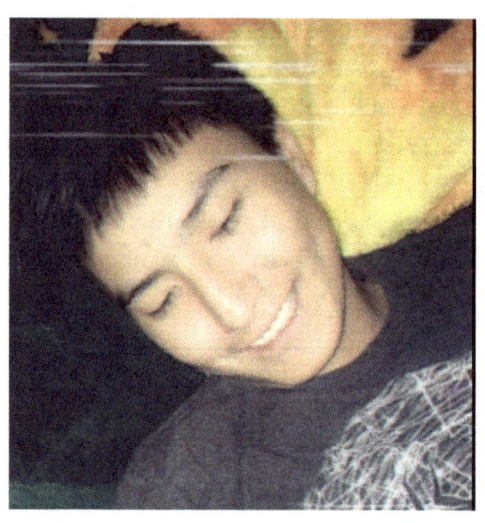

It's been really hard to keep strong. But I am trying my best. This year will be hard for me, seeing the prom pics, graduation next week… My son would have turned 18 next week. It's hard for me, because my son would have been doing all of it. So to all the students and teachers that went to school with my son, Alize Allen Millard, please think of my son.

We will be celebrating your birthday for you, Son. It's gonna be a hard day for us. You will never be forgotten, my boy. I know you are always looking after all of us. We will never give up on getting justice for you, my boy. Just know you are truly, deeply loved by your family. We miss you each and every day.

It's hard not seeing you. We miss your voice and your beautiful smile. Just know you are not forgotten, and we miss you more than words could say. My heart is shattered into a million pieces. It will never the same without you. We love you so much!

Jamie Millard
*Photo courtesy of Jamie Millard

Jon William Rice
South Dakota Ties
Unsolved Death

Personal note: I knew Jon Rice from high school, Washington Sr High School, Sioux Falls, SD, class of 1976. I didn't know him well, but what I did know, I admired. He was charismatic, smart, gregarious, and popular. Arguably handsome with his fluffy, golden curls, his muscular, track-fit legs, and wide smile, he caught the eye of more than his deserved share of girls. I knew whatever he did with his future, as with all those popular kids I admired in high school, it was going to be important, probably dramatic, and patently unforgettable. I was heartbroken to know it would be his premature, mysterious, and brutal death that would fulfill that prediction. I believe, and will forever, that his murder was not the result of something nefarious with which he was involved, but a craven act upon a beautiful young man who was trying to do the right thing.

On Friday, March 11, 1984, Jon Rice got a ride home from a friend at their work, First Wyoming Bank in Jackson, WY. They'd made plans to go for a Saturday morning jog before Jon's race that Saturday afternoon.

The next morning, his co-worker found Jon's condominium door ajar, entered, and found Jon dead. He'd been shot execution style in the back of the head, his hands and feet bound. Authorities found Jon's wallet, open to his ID, nearby. The room had been ransacked.

The murder weapon, a .22 pump action rifle belonging to his roommate, Gary Gilbert, was found on the mattress nearby. Authorities stated that multiple guns belonging to Gilbert were found pulled from underneath Gilbert's bed, and that his room was also torn apart. They state that the place was "taken apart as if someone were looking for something." There was no evidence of forced entry.

Witnesses claim to have seen someone leaving Jon's condo at around 1:44 a.m. that morning, and a neighbor stated that she heard a "ruckus" somewhere between midnight and 3:00 a.m.,= but didn't hear a gunshot.

Jon had worked as a credit officer at the now-defunct First Wyoming Bank in Jackson. He shared his condo at Twinberry Condominiums on Highway 390 in Teton County with Gilbert. Gilbert was away in Casper, WY, at the time of Jon's death, in the process of buying a boat, and was eliminated as a suspect.

Initially, law enforcement suspected that his death was the result of a messy love triangle, as he was known as a "ladies man," but those theories dwindled upon further investigation.

They also suspected drugs might have been involved with Jon's murder, having found traces of marijuana and cocaine in the apartment. Law enforcement officials wondered if Jon had been mistaken for his roommate. With the wallet lying out, open to his ID, it appeared as though Jon had removed it to prove who he was to the assailants. Though others saw the resemblance between Jon and his roommate, Gilbert did not believe he looked like Rice and discounted this theory.

Another theory law enforcement investigated was Jon's connection to an investigation he was helping with on behalf of the bank of a Jackson lawyer, Cabell Venable, who was later indicted, in 1985, for stealing around $1.5

million from multiple citizens. According to witnesses, Jon Rice, Venable, and a restaurateur named Ehlers had been in a meeting weeks before Rice was killed. Venable had helped Ehlers start a local restaurant organization. Jon had apparently told his roommate at one point that he had "stuff in a briefcase that would blow the bank wide open." There is no mention in any articles stating if that briefcase or its contents were ever found or what that information might be.

Witnesses told authorities that Jon had frequented Venable's gambling den at a restaurant he owned on the edge of town, and that Venable had a reputation for being involved with drugs. After Venable was sentenced for embezzlement and later paroled, he moved to Florida to practice law and eventually died, offering no answers to authorities regarding these theories.

It came to the authorities' attention later in the investigation that Jon and Gilbert shared a safe-deposit box, which contained $30,000. It was found to be Gilbert's money, which he withdrew, and he later left town.

Adding to the mystery surrounding Jon's murder was the death of multiple people around the same time as Jon's death, dating between October 1983 and June 1984.

On the same day as Jon's death, a business associate of Jon's, Stanley Kerr, a landowner in Jackson, was shot and killed in Florida. After investigation, Kerr's wife, her lover, and a hired hit man were all tried and convicted of his murder.

Another of Jon's acquaintances, though distant, 27-year-old Lisa Ehlers, wife of the restaurateur, was found shot dead in June of 1984 along Highway 191 in Sublette County, WY. She'd also rented a safe-deposit box at the bank where Jon worked. But 25 years after her murder, a man by the name of Troy D. Willoughby was found guilty of her murder. He claimed she'd left a party early in the morning hours without paying for her drugs. He followed her, got her to pull over, and shot her.

And the last, though his connection to Jon is tenuous because they didn't run in the same social circle, is that of Eric James Cooper. Cooper was last seen on October 14, 1983, at the Highlander Bar in Jackson. His skull was found on August 14, 1986, by hikers on Signal Mountain with a .22 caliber bullet inside, the shot to the back of his head. His shallow grave was found nearby. He had told Jackson lawyer, W. Keith Goody, before he went missing that he was going to "try to handle this," alluding to something he was involved with that might be a danger to him. It's suspected that he was involved with drugs, perhaps acting as an informant. This crime is still unsolved.

With those deaths all occurring in an eight-month period in a town of only 4,500 residents in 1984, the temptation for law enforcement to believe they were connected was natural. But as the years and subsequent investigations went on, it seemed more of an eerie and unfortunate coincidence.

Jon's murder is still unsolved.

For your consideration:
~ Authorities found no evidence of forced entry, and the murder likely occurred at 1:44 a.m. Did Jon know his killer and let him or her in? And when? If not, how did he or she enter without force?

~ If Jon's murder was planned, why was his roommate's gun used to kill him? Is it possible the killer knew the guns were there, or was this an impulsive act? Wouldn't someone intending to kill Jon bring his own weapon with him?

~ With the condo being trashed, was it always the killer's plan to kill Jon and ransack the condo to find whatever they were looking for? Or were they hoping the condo was empty? Were they surprised to find him there?

~ Is it possible that this was a case of mistaken identity?

~ Why is there no mention of the briefcase and the potentially explosive contents Jon spoke of? Was it found, and if so, what information was in it?

If you know anything about the murder of Jon William Rice, please contact
 Jackson City Police Department at (307) 733-1430
 Or Teton County Sheriff's Office at (307) 733-2331
 Or submit an anonymous tip to Jackson Hole
 CrimeStoppers at (307) 733-5148.

(Ref: *Casper Star-Tribune; KELOLAND News; Planet Jackson Hole; Jackson Hole News and Guide; The Cowboy Picayune-Sunny Times*)

Jon Rice was born in Honolulu, Hawaii, before it was a state and died in Jackson, Wyoming, and in-between, his life was overflowing. To say he lived his short life to the fullest is an understatement.

He was the Emcee of Life! Always the fun one, making people laugh, introducing others to the adventures he so enjoyed.

He ran marathons, in fact he was supposed to run one the next morning...but instead he was murdered in his condo in Jackson...case still unsolved.

He coached the girls' softball team in Jackson. He was an avid skier, hiker, and lover of the out of doors.

He was smart, witty, and could always make my mom laugh, no matter what he had been up to...

When he applied for a job at the bank, he had a lengthy discussion about how the Federal Reserve System worked and they hired him on the spot.

We miss him, wonder what if? And most of all, why? Much love to you Jon...

Linda (Jon's sister)

A Good Friend: Jon Rice

Jon was one of those guys that had all kinds of friends, from the childhood buddies, high school to college. He had a unique personality that he had the ability to talk to most anyone. What a great person he was!

I remember when I left for the Army for 4 years, which seemed like an eternity but when I got out of the Army, I then headed to USD to school. I asked around Vermillion if Jon was still around and sure enough, he was. It was like I had never left.

He was a driven guy, we used to run 5-10 miles a day from downtown Vermillion to the Missouri River every morning. If I was ahead he couldn't handle it, he'd try the Rice talking method, to distract me so he could slide by me like I never noticed he tried anything to win. But JR loved to win!

He was the type of friend that if you had a flat tire at 3am in the morning and called him he'd come and help you. So once you became his friend, you knew it was for life.

Jeff Maschino

Donna Ann Lass
Missing Person

Donna Lass, originally from Beresford, SD, moved to South Lake Tahoe, CA, from the Bay Area near San Francisco in June of 1970. She worked as a registered nurse in the first aid room of the Sahara Tahoe Hotel & Casino in Stateline, Nevada. She had recently rented an apartment at the Monte Verdi on Pioneer Trail in South Lake Tahoe, a mere seven minutes away, and had only spent one night there before she went missing.

Donna had worked the evening of September 5th, 1970, scheduled to work into the early morning hours of September 6th. At 1:30 a.m., she made a log entry just before her last patient entered the room 15 minutes later, half an hour before she was to get off duty.

She was scheduled to make a log entry at 1:45 a.m., but that log entry was never completed. Her car was later found at her apartment, but she was never seen leaving the casino. Though all of her other personal belongings were found in her apartment, her purse and the clothing she was wearing that day were not found.

The next day, an unknown male called her landlord and her boss stating that Donna would not be returning due to a family emergency. The call was determined to be a hoax, and no trace of Donna was ever found again.

At one time, Donna's disappearance was suspected as being one of the Zodiac Killer's crimes, though the details of her disappearance didn't fit the serial killer's profile. A postcard mailed to detectives contained information implying the Zodiac Killer was responsible, but it was later found to have been forged by an investigator.

Officer Harvey Hines, a retired detective from Groveland, CA, stated in a September 2000 article in the *Los Angeles Times* that be believed she was abducted by someone at work. He stated that she left behind personal items including an opened letter and a dirty uniform, and that "on her log, a pen was dragged from the last word she wrote to the bottom of the page."

Donna's mother, Frances, and her sister, Mary, had visited Donna just before she went missing, and had gone back home to South Dakota. It was two weeks after Donna had gone missing before the family was informed of her disappearance. A friend of Donna's had called to say Donna hadn't shown up at work. The weekend Donna went missing happened to be the same weekend that a friend of Donna's had gone to Lake Tahoe to visit her but found that she wasn't there.

After the family learned that Donna was missing, her mother and sister, Mary, left for California to search for her. They hired a private investigator, and eventually, not finding her, they packed up all of Donna's belongings and drove her car home to South Dakota.

Donna was born November 3, 1944, and was 25 years old when she disappeared. She was 5'4" and weighed approximately 135 pounds. She is Caucasian with frosted blonde hair and blue eyes.

For your consideration:
~ How can the call to Donna's landlord and employer be considered a hoax? How would *anyone* know that Donna was missing so soon after she disappeared, other than the person responsible? How thoroughly was this call investigated? Did they ever determine who made the call?

~ How did Donna's car arrive at her home when no one saw her leave the casino? Did she happen to leave without anyone seeing her, make it home, and *then* she was abducted?

~ Since her purse is gone, but her car was still at her apartment, is it possible she simply left her home with someone she knew? Perhaps to go out for breakfast or drinks, and this person she knew was responsible for her disappearance?

~ Is it coincidence that she'd only spent one night in her new apartment before going missing? Could her disappearance have anything to do with current or past tenants in the building?

~ Was someone she worked with at the casino responsible for her disappearance? How else would she be able to leave the casino premises without being spotted, if it wasn't for someone who might know the best (most hidden) routes to take?

~ Was she forcibly abducted during her last log entry, accounting for her "dragged" pen marking? How, then, do you explain the opened letter and the dirty uniform at her home?

~ Was the opened letter and the dirty uniform left behind by her on the day of her disappearance? Were they left at work or at her home? Did she make it back home or did her abductor drive her car there? If it's the latter, why bother?

If you know anything about the disappearance of Donna Ann Lass, please contact
The South Lake Tahoe Police Department at (530) 542-6100

Or the Lake Tahoe Secret Witness Hotline at (530) 541-6800.

Photo courtesy of Patricia Teeman
(Ref: *South Tahoe Now; Los Angeles Times*; The Charley Project; Patricia Teeman)

I am Donna's older sister. There were eight children in our family, and Donna was the baby. Growing up, we looked out for her, though she was always quite capable.

We lived on a farm near Beresford in our younger days, and we all helped out. Even though Donna was 13 years younger than me, we had a lot of fun together. We had two brothers, but it was us six girls who were close and joked around. We worked together, we all had chores, but we had a good time.

After I left to get married and started having children, Donna and our other sister, Karen, helped me with the babies. They were so helpful.

We didn't see each other as much after I married and moved to Sioux Falls, but I know she helped Mom out quite a bit with the chores, sewing, etc. She enjoyed high school and loved joking around with her friends.

When Donna moved to California to be near our brother, Ray, she called to talk to our folks quite often. I'll never forget how worried our mom was when she hadn't heard from Donna after Labor Day. Mom had just been to visit Donna in California, and got home before Labor Day, and that was the last time she spoke to Donna.

It was so hard on our parents to lose Donna. It was hard on us all—something we never truly got over. And now, most of our family is gone. It's just my sister, Jo, and me. We think of her often and miss her terribly.

Patricia Teeman

Donna Lass was a classmate of mine at Beresford High School, graduating in 1962. It was the winter of 1961-62 that we had a wicked blizzard in SD and we were walking in the streets downtown with mounds of snow as high as the buildings.

We were confused as to what the next step would be after graduation. This is a time when there were no federal educational loan programs and thus finances were an issue. I was the oldest of ten children and Donna was I think the youngest of eight children. That night we decided that we would apply for nursing school. We were both accepted with neither of making a visit to the school.

We graduated from St. Joseph's Mercy School of Nursing in 1965. We were blessed that we both loved nursing, so it was a good choice. She was excellent nurse, very compassionate and kind, and her clinical skills were recognized by peers and faculty.

As I remember, Donna went to the west coast to work, and later worked near Lake Tahoe. That is where two friends from nursing school were to meet her in a hotel lobby at Lake Tahoe. Donna never met them and that was when they notified police to try to locate her. She had been working at the Sahara Tahoe Casino First Aid Station and her last charting entry was at 1:50 AM on September 6, 1970. Much information regarding her disappearance has been published and there was suspicion that she was murdered by the Zodiac killer.

After more than 50 years later she is still noted as "missing" and no remains have ever been found. Her family and especially her mother were devastated from this event and spent much money attempting to find out more information.

Donna was a delightful person, so full of life, and her

laughter was infectious. She made friends easily and was well liked by classmates. We did have a gathering of nursing classmates in Minneapolis a few years after graduation, and I remember that Donna had lost a lot of weight and was absolutely gorgeous. She was apparently very happy living on the west coast.

High school classmates, as well as nursing colleagues had much difficulty accepting her loss, and always remembered her at reunions. She apparently left this world, after caring for others at the first aid station. We have lost a friend, classmate, daughter, sister and excellent nurse. She is gone but will never be forgotten.

Rosemary Mullin, friend

Mariah High Hawk
Unsolved Death
Closed Without Closure

Though law enforcement officials have issued a statement saying that Mariah's death has been ruled as exposure, or hypothermia, the family disputes those claims. Whether or not law enforcement's claims are provable and true, circumstances surrounding this case leave too many questions to ignore. The goal in including this case in the book is to bring attention to it in case more evidence or details arise.

Mariah Angel High Hawk, 20, was a pretty mother of two young children, who lived with her children and her parents, Delbert High Hawk and Arlene White Crane-High Hawk in an apartment on the 1500 block of Kellogg Place in Rapid City, SD.

On Friday, February 12, 2016, between 7 and 7:30 p.m., Mariah and her boyfriend, Andrew, had a disagreement at her apartment. He left, telling her father that he was leaving because Mariah was texting another male. After he walked out of the apartment, Mariah followed in an effort to get her phone back from her boyfriend. When she left, she was in her stocking feet and without a coat, apparently anticipating only following him a short distance to retrieve her phone. She followed her boyfriend, going southwest from the apartment.

According to Delbert, Mariah's daughter, Mataya, had told him that Andrew had struck Mariah in the eye and it was bleeding. He then woke Arlene and told her about it, and concerned, they called "dispatch" and were told that she was an adult, and old enough to make her own decisions. They were then told, he says, that if she didn't return within 72 hours, to call back. He claimed that he and Arlene and other family members called and texted her, but got no reply.

The next day, Delbert claims he contacted the hospital and police station inquiring about the whereabouts of Mariah, but no one had seen her. He drove around looking for her but didn't find her, hoping that there was a simple explanation, that maybe she and her boyfriend gone to a motel or somewhere to hang out until they both had to work on Monday.

On Sunday, February 14, around 3:20 p.m., police responded to a call about a deceased female found underneath a utility trailer at 1220 Silverleaf Avenue. While police are on the scene investigating the death, Delbert arrived having heard of a deceased female, and told the detective about his missing daughter. He was then taken to the morgue where he positively identified his daughter Mariah.

Police state that Mariah was last seen walking down the hill from 302 St. Cloud Street, an area between her house on Kellogg Place, from where she left, and Silverleaf Avenue, where she was found deceased.

In a police report issued to the *Rapid City Journal* about Mariah's case, they state, "It should be noted that at no point in Ms. Highhawk's disappearance was she reported to police as missing by friends or family."

After an autopsy was performed, police issued a statement saying that Mariah died from exposure, or hypothermia. At the time of her disappearance, the weather in Rapid City was freezing with rain turning to snow.

Multiple news reports aired over the following months about Mariah's death and her family's dissatisfaction with their findings. According to police, medical examinations determined that, although she had numerous marks on her body, the marks came from decomposition, and there were no injuries to Mariah that would have caused her death.

Delbert stated that initially, he received word from police and medical officials that no drugs or substances were found in Mariah's system at the time of her autopsy, other than trace amounts of a prescription she was taking. He also stated that she didn't drink, smoke, or do drugs, and was very proud of herself for that. He claimed that later, those findings had changed and they had indeed found drugs in her system that may have impeded her judgment, disorienting her, and contributing to her death. They believe Mariah was disoriented due to the drugs in her system and being cold, and sought shelter under the trailer for warmth.

Photos taken by the family of Mariah at her funeral clearly show multiple contusions on her face, arms, and hands, including a laceration on Mariah's head. Medical officials stated that "autopsies are not kind" to the human body, and that those marks are a part of decomposition.

Family members shared information as well, stating that they saw a boot or foot print on Mariah's hoodie sweatshirt, on the upper back/shoulder area. That sweatshirt was thrown away and not given back to the family, according to Delbert. They also claimed that several texts from family members were erased from Mariah's phone before the police retrieved it from Mariah's boyfriend. Mariah's family claimed that there was a disturbance reported the night before her body was found, in that same area.

Mariah's case is considered closed by law enforcement, but in a statement in a *KOTA TV* interview, police said they are "always willing to take another look at the case," and they encourage anyone who might know something about the case to come forward.

For your consideration:

~ The area where Mariah was found is mere blocks from where she lived and close to other residences. Why wouldn't Mariah seek shelter at a house or simply walk home? Were the drugs in her system significant enough to have caused her to become this disoriented?

~ What of the reports of a disturbance in the area where Mariah was found? Is it possible she didn't crawl under the trailer but was placed there? Why would she seek shelter under a trailer, of all places?

~ The medical examiner stated that there were no injuries that caused Mariah's death. Is it possible for a person who was severely beaten to go into shock, be stuffed under a trailer, and then succumb to the cold?

~ What of the differing claims that one toxicology report said there were no drugs or substances found in Mariah's system, and later, another that said there were? Which is it?

~ Several news reports state that temps were freezing along with rain turning to snow. In online searches of the weather that day in Rapid City, timeanddate.com and wunderground.com state that the rain had stopped by 6 p.m. on Friday night, and the temps ranged from 25-30 degrees at midnight, to a high of 52 degrees at noon on Saturday. Temps on Saturday night were between 27 and 39 degrees. When did Mariah seek shelter under the trailer? What was her time of death? Were the temps severe enough for her to seek shelter under a trailer rather than walk the 5-10 minutes back home?

~ How fast does a body decompose in the previously stated temps? What can be made of the very obvious marks on her hands and face?

~ Can a second, independent autopsy be done to expand on some of these findings or provide more information, to give the family more clarification?

If you know anything about the death of Mariah High Hawk, please contact the

Rapid City Police Department at (605) 394-4131

Or to submit an anonymous tip, text RCPD and your tip to 847411.

(Ref: *KOTA TV; Rapid City Journal*; Justice for Mariah High Hawk Facebook page; Delbert High Hawk; *KNBN NewsCenter1*)

"I will do anything." ~ *Delbert High Hawk, father of Mariah High Hawk*

These four words Delbert first spoke to me in our talks about Mariah left an indelible mark on my heart. The emotion he conveyed in them seem to express the collective anguish of all those left behind after a tragedy such as this.

Mariah liked to joke around. She loved to help out—she never complained, wasn't afraid to pitch in, and always in the center of whatever needed to be done. She loved and respected the elderly, enjoyed cooking for them, and they loved her. She dreamed of becoming a registered nurse.

When she was 8 years old, she began dancing jingle dress. At age 13 or 14, she tried traditional Native dance, but went back to jingle dress. "Jingle dress is my way," she said. She enjoyed sports, especially basketball, in school. She was smart

and always worked to improve herself. She was proud that she was against drugs and alcohol. She was a good mama to her daughter, Mataya, and her son, Roman.
   Delbert High Hawk

   *Photo courtesy of Gwen Reddest

Ellabeth Lodermeier
Missing Person

March 7, 1974, authorities in Sioux Falls, SD, received a call from Community Services Offices employees stating that their co-worker, Ellabeth Lodermeier, had not shown up for work. That morning, her concerned co-workers and estranged husband went to her home to investigate. Her door was locked and her car was in the driveway. Upon entering, they found bread dough on the kitchen counter that had risen and fallen. They also found a partially eaten pizza and spilled flour on the floor, but no trace of Ellabeth. Law enforcement arrived at her home at 305 North Indiana Avenue and began the investigation, noting that the scene suggested she was forcibly abducted. Gene told investigators that he had last seen Ellabeth on March 6th. The only items that appeared to be missing from her home were her jacket and her purse.

Ellabeth Lodermeier, 25, had recently filed for divorce from Gene Lodermeier, citing allegations of abuse, which was also witnessed by friends and family. She'd married Gene in January of 1970 in Aberdeen where he attended Northern State University. After he'd graduated, they settled in Sioux Falls, and she attended college at Augustana. She graduated with her degree in social work from Augustana in 1972. She filed for divorce in 1973 and disappeared three weeks before the divorce became final. Online sources vary in their reports about whether Gene and Ellabeth lived together at the home on North Indiana.

When Ellabeth didn't show up for days and weeks, her coworker offered a $1200 reward for information on Ellabeth's whereabouts, but no information came in.

Months pass without any movement in the case until seven months later when Ellabeth's credit cards showed up in women's restroom at the Canadian National Railway in Dauphin, Manitoba, Canada. Authorities believe they were placed there to throw off the investigation. No leads emerged from the discovery, however, and the case went cold.

Six years later, in November of 1980, six Sioux Falls police were acquitted of harassment charges that Gene Lodermeier had filed, accusing them of targeting him over Ellabeth's disappearance.

In January of 1989, Gene Lodermeier was sentenced to 45 years in prison for grand theft for stealing construction equipment. He served 13 years and was paroled in 2002. He was never charged in Ellabeth's disappearance. Gene died at his home in 2013 of an aortic aneurysm at the age of 66.

On February 21, 2000, before Gene's release, Gene Lodermeier, and the Justice for Gene Lodermeier group, penned an open letter to the public stating his case that the charges of grand theft were manufactured. Among the many claims he made in this letter, he addressed the theft, stating that the property he was accused of stealing was stored in an abandoned building on property he owned but was rented by a tenant, and that he wasn't even present when it was stored there. He states his family and employees stored the property. He lists several claims of improprieties and misconduct by his defense attorney and the judge involved in his case, citing their refusal to recuse themselves due to their personal involvement with Ellabeth. (Ref: *Argus Leader*, October 29, 2000)

The only other clue to Ellabeth's disappearance surfaced

in 1992 when a farmer discovered Ellabeth's purse, wallet, and checkbook east of Sioux Falls along the Big Sioux River. Over the years, several tips have come in to authorities, but no solid leads have emerged in her disappearance.

When Ellabeth was last seen, she was wearing a blue peacoat, blue sweatshirt, and blue jeans. She was born November 26, 1948, is 5'1" and 105 pounds with brown hair and green eyes. Her nickname is Beth and her maiden name is Keller.

For your consideration:
~ How many of the claims Gene made in his letter can be verified?
~ Is 45 years for grand theft an exorbitantly long sentence for grand theft? Was Gene unfairly accused?
~ If not Gene, then who could have abducted her? Could this be a random act? Or was it someone Ellabeth knew?
~ How is it possible that Ellabeth's purse and checkbook show up along the river after 18 years? Were these items also placed there to throw off investigators?
~ Why would Gene admit to seeing Ellabeth the night before? Did they live together? Did neighbors see him there?

If you know anything about the disappearance of Ellabeth Lodermeier, please contact the Sioux Falls Police Department at (605) 367-7234
Or submit an anonymous tip to CrimeStoppers at (877) 367-7007.

(Ref: *Argus Leader; KELOLAND News*; The Charley Project; *DakotaNewsNow*)

I was young, so I just remember Ellabeth's beautiful smile, and how pretty she was. She was very sweet, kind, and easy going. I just remember her being a caring person. Her disappearance was very hard on my family. Not being able to have closure was hard, along with not knowing what happened. It still bothers us. Not being able to find her body is another issue that bothers us. We would love to know where she is so we can bury her next to my grandparents.

Liz Crow, Ellabeth's niece

Ellabeth worked hard restoring her home, furthering her education, and spending time with family. She took me to the movies, the beach, and answered my endless questions.

She was always wanting to help people that were less fortunate than she. She was pursuing a career in social services—so many needy families lost out on her caring personality. She dreamed of having a good marriage and family.

Her disappearance had an impact in all our lives; it's the not knowing what happened to her. There is no closure, which was extremely difficult for our grandparents (Ellie's parents), and our mother (Ellie's sibling).

She was kind, caring, and easy going. We miss her smile and her laughter.

Kristie Jacobson, Ellabeth's niece

*Photo courtesy of Elizabeth Crow

The Cruelty of Closure

Definition of Closure by Merriam-Webster: 1 : an act of *closing* : the condition of being closed *closure* of the eyelids business *closures* the *closure* of the factory. 2 : an often comforting or satisfying sense of finality victims needing *closure* also : something (such as a satisfying ending) that provides such a sense.

Closure can be the cruelest of words, alluding to a promise it can't keep—hope of life returning to normal, answers that satisfy, reasons, a settled heart, peace of mind, justice, perhaps forgiveness, finality, and moving forward. Happiness.

Some might even say that closure is retribution in the absence of legal justice or answers. An eye for an eye. Hardly ideal. Nor legal. But the idea of closure is not up for debate; it's personal to and for only those who've lost someone to violence or suspicious circumstances; those who seek answers.

To those who have never experienced a loss to which there were little or no answers, the word might imply something akin to the banging shut of a depressing book, the slamming of a heavy door to a dark mystery, slapping the dust off our hands after an arduous job and saying, "Done."

But many who speak of closure from personal experience testify that even after years and years of work and persistence and torturous emptiness and yearning, and they finally saw justice, answers, or resolution, it still wasn't over. The all-consuming search didn't come to a screeching halt. The person they'd been fighting for is still gone. How could there ever be true closure when *nothing* would ever be the same? The world is different; their life is different. Forever.

We all know there's no end to grief. It doesn't leave. It imbeds itself in us, and we grow around it. And because it doesn't leave, because it's always there, like the tiniest metal shard, and without rhyme or reason, it zings us, reminds us, "I'm still here."

Can someone seeking closure reach a point where they have no more questions? What led to the incident? Did my loved one suffer? Was anyone else involved? And the one question whose answer, if given, will never be adequate or sufficiently understood: *Why?* No reason could ever be great enough to fill the black, bottomless chasm of grief and anger before us.

And to be fair, for those who have lost someone to violence or disappearance, maybe closure—however ambiguous or untenable—is all they have left for which to hope. It's a kind of goal that, once reasonably within reach, might yet remain out of reach, like climbing mountain after mountain, hoping for that perfect view. A feeling. A notion. A sense of some kind of ending. But a goal, nonetheless, because it has purpose and meaning.

One would imagine closure is different for everyone: reaching that place and finding *something* . . . perhaps a place where it doesn't hurt as much as the moment before. And maybe that's enough to get through today.

Jean Janis
Unsolved Death

On January 11, 1989, Jean Janis, a 46-year-old mother of five, was found dead in the North Platte River in Scottsbluff, NE. According to her daughter, Ang, the day after Jean was discovered, a newspaper article was published stating a local Indian woman committed suicide by drowning, mentioning that she was an alcoholic, an unnecessary and cruel addendum, which angered family members.

Ang states that many years later, Jean's family was contacted by cold case investigators, saying Jean hadn't drowned because there was no water found in her lungs, and bruises were found all over her body. Family members and certain law enforcement officials have suspects in mind, but lacking evidence, there is little anyone can do in the way of seeking justice.

Jean's death is still unsolved.

If you know anything about Jean Janis's death, please contact

Scottsbluff Police Department at (308) 632-7176

Or submit an anonymous tip at Scottsbluff CrimeStoppers at (308) 632-STOP (7867).

Photo courtesy of Ang Pru
(Ref: Ang Pru)

In loving memory of Jean Janis, beloved mother, grandmother, sister, aunt, and friend. Everyone who ever knew her say she was a kind, gentle, caring, and loving person. Never harming anyone, she had no enemies. Tragically murdered, 1-11-89, at the young age of 46. Her improbable death was not investigated, but insensitively reported by the authorities and media.

As a tribute, her family wishes that her inconceivable passing bring attention to the enormously high amount of especially Native women missing and murdered. The many different authorities must work together with the media and public to continually investigate the many unresolved cases that plague the underprivileged people of this country.

Cold case investigators are working to bring closure to her case and reveal the truth. She will forever be in our hearts and always in our thoughts.

Rachel Lucille Cyriacks
Missing Person

November 14th was Mary Schabot's birthday, and when she didn't hear from her daughter, Rachel, she knew something had to be wrong.

On November 13, 2013, Rachel Cyriacks, 30, had driven to a correctional facility near Huron, SD, to pick up her husband, Brad Cyriacks, from jail where he had been incarcerated on a domestic violence incident a few days earlier. He had pleaded guilty to violating a protection order and spent a week in jail.

Rachel's husband later told investigators that she picked him up at a nearby gas station. He had gone to the gas station after being released from jail and called her from there to have her pick him up there. He told authorities that they left the gas station, they drove the 20 minutes to their home, and then she drove him to the home of a friend, Travis Griffith, in Huron. She dropped him off and that was the last time he saw her.

Rachel and Brad had a history with drug abuse and a stormy relationship, and their three children were being cared for by relatives at the time of her disappearance. Rachel had found work at a local dog food plant, Performance Pet, and was in the process of filing for divorce and seeking custody of her children. She had also filed for a temporary protective order against Brad for abuse, but that protection order was dismissed when Rachel failed to show up in court. She had hoped to put her life back together.

Though Mary states that it wasn't unusual not to hear from Rachel for days, when Mary didn't hear from her for over a week, especially when Rachel missed Mary's birthday, she became concerned and went to Rachel's house. She had a key, let herself in, and searched the home, but found nothing out of place.

She reported Rachel missing to authorities early on, but it wasn't until a month later that law enforcement launched a full-scale investigation into Rachel's disappearance.

Investigators determined by Rachel's cell phone records that she traveled from Woonsocket to Huron on November 13th, and also confirmed an incoming call from a gas station in Huron, near the jail where Brad was incarcerated. She'd received a voicemail while traveling through a "dead zone" and made an outgoing call to the gas station in Huron, where authorities believe she picked up Bradley.

There are no cell phone records of Rachel's whereabouts after she picked up Bradley in Huron, and authorities assume her phone was turned off after that.

There seems to be conflicting information about Bradley's claims: Rachel picked him up in Huron and dropped him off at Travis Griffith's, and that they drove home and then went to Travis Griffith's.

Investigators questioned multiple people in Rachel's disappearance and searched the area around Woonsocket and Huron with airplane surveillance, dive teams, and side-scan sonar technology when searching rivers and bodies of water. Area wells, abandoned buildings, junkyards, and bodies of water such as the James River, were all searched. Private search-and-rescue teams also participated in the hunt for clues as to Rachel's whereabouts. No trace of Rachel or her gray 1995 Chevy Silverado pickup was found.

Family and investigators also focused on a treasured green, pink, and white quilt owned by Rachel that was later found to be missing from her home. The quilt was never recovered.

In January of 2014, investigators discovered Rachel's pickup (seemingly) hidden behind a Quonset on a bee farm owned by Travis Griffith's family. There was extensive damage to the undercarriage, making it inoperable, and the drive train had been removed.

Investigators stated that Bradley gave a "half-story" about the pickup, saying they had been making repairs to the truck, and had no explanation about why the drive train had been pulled out of it. Nor could he explain how he was in possession of the pickup when he had previously told authorities that Rachel had dropped him off and driven away.

Though law enforcement are still in possession of the pickup, they state that they found the damaged undercarriage of interest, but that it didn't produce any valuable clues.

Rachel Lucille Cyriacks was 30-years-old at the time of her disappearance and was 5'5" tall and 130-140 pounds. She had dark blonde hair and hazel eyes and had numerous tattoos: one on her neck that says "Brad" in dark script; a blue playboy bunny logo on her left hip; a black tribal-type heart on her lower back; designs of two large red flowers; stars; a tree; and the initials "RJ" on her right forearm. Rachel has a dimple on her right cheek and surgical scars on her abdomen.

For your consideration:

~ Why would Bradley claim Rachel dropped him off, that he never saw her after that, but apparently had her pickup the entire time, or at the very least, knew that it was on the property of his friend, Travis?

~ Why was the undercarriage damaged? Is there a way to determine where, exactly, the vehicle had been through forensic testing?

~ With the damaged undercarriage and missing drive train, can one assume that the pickup had been through rough terrain? Might this be a clue as to where Rachel might be (IF Bradley was involved in her disappearance)?

~ What would the motive be for anyone, including Bradley, to harm Rachel? Is it possible that an accident, or accidental death, is responsible for her disappearance, and she was left somewhere out of fear and panic?

~ What might Travis know?

Relatives have offered a $1000 reward for information leading to Rachel's whereabouts.

If you know anything about the disappearance of Rachel Cyriacks, please contact

The Huron Police Department at (605) 353-8550

Or Sanborn County Sheriff's Office at (605) 796-4511

Or submit an anonymous tip at (605) 996-1700 (Mitchell CrimeStoppers).

(Ref: *InForum; Argus Leader;* The Charley Project; *KELOLAND News*; Mary Schabot)

Hi, Rachel ~

It has been way too long since I heard your voice or saw your face. The pain never goes away. Every moment is tough. Never gets any easier. If the wait does anything, it makes me mad. Mad that no one has said anything. Mad that they are getting away with this. I have to believe God will not have them. Hell will. My tears will never end or my trying to find you. Or maybe justice or closure.
Always loving and missing you,
Mom

*Photo courtesy of Mary Schabot

Charles "Charley Boy" Quiver Unsolved Death

On March 2, 2016, at approximately 2:30-3 a.m., Charley Boy Quiver and his nephew, Fred, awoke to a smoke-filled house. Fred rushed to gather his children, and when he couldn't get the door open, put them out a window.

He called for Charley Boy, his 83-year-old uncle, but couldn't find him and had to exit the window himself.

Family members stood by helplessly and repeatedly called the fire department, located 9/10 of a mile away from the burning home. As they watched in horror, the house became engulfed in flames, with Charley Boy still inside.

No help came for hours. It wasn't until days later that as Abbie (Bee), Charley's daughter, stated, the family was informed that the door to the home was padlocked from the outside and the fire was possibly arson. Charley Boy's body was found just inside that locked door.

(Sidenote: Charley Boy's son, Charles "Mesu" Quiver, was found murdered six months earlier in Rapid City. This unrelated case is as yet unsolved, and also included in this book.)

For your consideration:
~ Why do all accounts of this case say "suspected" arson, with a padlock on the exterior of the door, and not "arson and murder"? Was the padlock there before the fire? If not, was it placed on the door directly before the fire?

~ Was this attack on Charley Boy's house, his life, in retaliation for a crime that didn't involve him personally?

~ Was evidence of arson, such as an accelerant, found

on the outside of the house?

If you know anything about the death of Charley Boy Quiver, please contact
FBI's Minneapolis Field Office at (763) 569-8000.

(Ref: *Rapid City Journal;* Abbie "Bee" Quiver)

Charles "Charley Boy" Quiver

"DAD"

Charlie Boy Quiver "Dad" Loved and respected by ALL who knew him, where touched by his passion for life and devastated by his senseless death in a house fire on the Pine Ridge Indian Reservation.

DOB 12/04/1933 DOD 03/02/2016

Charlie Boy was born in a blizzard in Wanbli, SD, to James Jonas Quiver & Lucinda Richards Quiver was delivered at home on 12/04/1933. Married Elaine Quick Bear Quiver, had four daughter's Madonna, Francine, Abbie, Jerilyn, and one son Charles.

US Air Force – Korea "Home of the FREE because of the Brave"

Our father was a humble man, who enjoyed family, it didn't matter if we were related or not everyone was welcome to share a meal and visit. Our father loved to hunt, fish and be outdoors when we were growing up, he shared his game with everyone and delivered it too. Our mother was his rock, thru thick and thin it didn't matter they were a team and raised their children to make the best of things always and not dwell on things that would and could never be changed.

"Tragic" was said many times during the time of his death. I kept telling myself there is no definition for tragic, when our father burnt up in a house fire. At the time everyone repeatedly said call the fire department while we cried and watched in horror while a blazing hot fire took our father. That's the biggest joke of ALL! it's only $9/10^{th}$'s of a mile away. The Pine Ridge Indian Reservation has no structural fire department no one came for hours, it seem like we were in a time warp where time stood still for those precious moments when we realized there would be no more "dad." The real tragedy was that in later days we were told the door was padlocked from the outside and he was trapped in his own home.

We may never know who, someone is guilty but who, that spun in my mind for years. Does anyone even care? We as a family console each other, we visit about things, I know we all wish things could be different but in our hearts we know we have to rely on a higher power no one will ever confess…

One day our children will see our picture and ask "Who are these people?" and we will Smile with invisible tears because a heart is touched with a strong word and you will say: "It was them that I had the best days of my Life with!" <u>I don't know the Author of this quote but it's true!</u>

Bee Quiver

*Photo courtesy of Abbie Quiver

Pamela Dunn
Missing Person

On December 9, 2001, Pamela Jean Dunn arrived home, dropped off by her mother, Loretta Hallquist, around 6 p.m. At approximately 8 p.m., Pamela's daughter, Stacey Bensen, phoned Pamela to see if she had a phone number for a mutual acquaintance. Pamela said she did not have it, but that her ex-boyfriend, David Asmussen would know it. Stacey could hear Pamela speak with David in the background, and then explained to her daughter over the phone that David was picking up the last of his belongings from her home.

David and Pamela had a long-term, tumultuous relationship that ended in August of 2000. On August 25th, 2000, a protection order was issued against David Asmussen in Codington County, SD, for domestic abuse. The protection order prohibited David from "contact(ing) directly or indirectly, in any manner" Pamela, her daughter, Pamela's mother, any member of Pamela's family, employer, or co-workers. It also prohibited David from coming within 100 feet of any vehicle owned by Pamela Dunn. The court order was to stay in effect until August of 2003.

The same evening of December 9th, Pamela called her mother about 11 p.m. and told her that David had called her and sounded upset, like he was crying.

On December 10, 2001, Pamela failed to show up for work. Police went to Pamela's apartment and found Pamela's car parked outside, the door locked, her purse on the table. There were no signs of a disturbance, but Pamela was never found.

During the course of the ensuing investigation, David admitted to being at Pamela's residence and speaking with her by phone on December 8th and 9th of 2001. Law enforcement officials also found that Asmussen had made repeated calls—seventeen between November 25th and December 9th—to her residence and spoke with her on numerous occasions, all in violation of the protection order. Threatening and abusive messages on her voice messaging system from a male who did not identify himself were recovered, and those messages had been listened to and saved prior to Pamela's disappearance.

On February 6, 2002, a woman by the name of Penny Ries faced charges of forging a $200 check using Pamela's checking account. She was set to stand trial the following April. No other details were available on this case.

David Asmussen was arrested on three counts of stalking and violating a protection order. During the August 20, 2004, hearing, David Asmussen expressed his desire to dismiss his attorneys, insisting on representing himself, against the advice of counsel. He was subsequently found guilty of stalking Pamela Dunn and sentenced to 40 months. He was later tried for kidnapping in the case of Pamela Dunn and sentenced to life.

To this day, no trace of Pamela Dunn has been found. In the fall of 2020, a tip led investigators to dig up a well on an abandoned Deuel County farm in the hopes of finding Pamela's body. Human hair was discovered, but it was too degraded to test for DNA matches. Bones were also discovered, but were found not to be human.

Though David was never tried in her death, and rumors circulated that Pamela could have gone to Florida, authorities consider her disappearance suspicious, considering the circumstances involved. David has been asked several times to disclose the location of her body if he knows, but has never cooperated.

Pamela Jean Dunn was born October 4, 1963, and was 38 at the time of her disappearance. She was 5'2" tall and 135 pounds. She has brown hair and brown eyes. She has pierced ears, surgical scars from a hysterectomy on her abdomen, and a discolored scar under her nose. Pam's nickname is Curly.

For your consideration:

~ Who is Penny Ries in relation to Pamela Dunn or David Asmussen? Where did she get Pamela's account information or Pamela's checkbook, if that was her means of forgery? What became of Penny Ries?

~ Why would David Asmussen insist on representing himself? To get a mistrial?

~ What connections did David have with the abandoned farm that authorities dug up?

~ If that was human hair they found on the abandoned farm, could there be more evidence there?

~ Is there anyone who can convince David to reveal what he knows about Pamela's disappearance? What, if anything, does he know?

~ There has to be someone else who knows what happened to Pamela. Doesn't there?

If you know anything about the disappearance of Pamela Dunn, please contact

Watertown Police Department at (605) 882-6210

Or the Department of Criminal Investigation at (605)

773-3331
Or the Codington County Sheriff at (605) 882-6280
Or submit an anonymous tip at https://codingtonsheriff.com/tip-line/

(Ref: *KELOLAND News*; STATE v. ASMUSSEN; The Charley Project)

My mom was one of the happiest, friendliest, caring people you could ever meet she would do almost anything for someone that was in need of help.

One of her biggest passions was her job at "Jenkins Nursing Home" it was her dream to help people, she loved her residents. Even on her days off, she would have to make a quick stop to check on her residents and to say hi. She adored them as well as her co-workers.

Another one of her passions were collecting angels. She had over 200 of them and every one of them, she said, represents someone in her life, even loved ones that we have lost. My mom lost my sister when my sister was 5 years old. I was 2 years old at the time. She died from an elevator accident that was very hard on my mom. I don't remember much, but I would hear my mom crying about it at times.

My mom enjoyed spending time with her family (me and her two grandkids and my mom's mom my grandma, Lorretta). We would watch movies, play some UNO, listen to country music, even sit at my grandma's and watch "The Price is right" and following after that "The Young and the restless." Those were the days. I call them my happy days. Everyone was here and we all got together for the holidays.

My best memories of my mom was when I first found out I was pregnant with my first baby I was very young, I was 14 years old, and being 14 not knowing how she was going to react was scary. At first she was upset and very emotional, and worried about my schooling. And wondering how I was gonna be able to be a mommy, go to school, and still be able to be a kid myself. One day she looked at me hugged me and said everything will work out and she was gonna be there for me all the way and to help me. And she did. I was very blessed to have such a great mom who didn't put me down because I was pregnant or try to talk me into adoption. She stood next to me through a lot of hard times in my life. She never gave up on me or turned her back on me.

Her and I were very close we had a very strong bond. She was my best friend I could tell her everything, even if it was about boys lol. She was a fantastic Grandma. Her and my oldest were very close. Then when I turned 18, I was pregnant with my second baby so I graduated high school with 2 daughters, and a very happy mom.

My second daughter was pretty little when my mom went missing. She was a little over a year old. She didn't get much time with her like my first one did and that breaks my heart, like now I have had 7 babies and 5 of them will never be able to get that chance to meet their Grandma and it hurts me everyday. When my kids will say they wish they could have met her, I have told them some funny stories of her and I and showed them pictures of her and I tell them every day that she would be so proud of them and that she loves them just as much as I do. Also that she watches over them to make sure they are safe and that they are being good.

My fourth baby was a boy his name was Joel he was 3 weeks and 6 days old he passed away from SIDS on Oct 4th of 2004, which was also my mom's birthday. I didn't think I was gonna make it through that loss. And at a time like that a girl needs her mom and my mom was gone. I hit bottom I didn't want to go another day of this journey of my life but I still had my grandma, my mom's mom, and she held me and told me to stay strong. And that my mom was there next to me, and if I gave up what are my other kids going to do without their mom. And she was right. I had to stay strong for my other kids it wasn't easy.

There are still days that just seem so emotional and hard to breathe, but I keep going one day at a time. In 2012 I lost my grandma, my mom's mom, due to cancer. Nobody knew she was sick, and I was a mess—a complete mess. I was losing the last part of my mom I still can't get over the day I sat at the hospital with my uncles and aunts listening to a doctor telling us how sick my grandma was, and she maybe had a week. I fell to my knees and cried and cried. I'm the type of person that doesn't understand death I don't deal with it very well at all.

My mom's disappearance has made a big impact on my life I can tell you that I don't think anyone could have prepared me for the emptiness that I felt when I got the phone call stating my mom never showed up for work. My heart instantly dropped. I had that feeling something was wrong cause the day before she was telling me about a very threaetning message Dave had left on her voice mail.

Dave and her had a very rocky relationship. My mom and I ended up putting protection orders on him. He was a crazy man. Anyway after I hung up with the police officer, I ran outside of the place I was at, and just started crying, hoping my mom was ok, and just over slept which she never did.

No one could have helped me be ready for this the unfortunate reality that this feeling and what I was gonna go through would ever go away. The loss of my mom has created such a void that will never be filled. The worst part of this void (the emptiness) is that I am reminded of it constantly. Especially holidays my mom's favorite holiday was Christmas, almost everything triggers it. The pain, the hurt that was brought unto me on the day my mom disappeared has been one of the most difficult parts of my grief journey. It is a part of my life that will never heal.

If there is one thing I have learned throughout this "grief journey," it's that everyone has their opinions. Their advice and their feelings on relating to what I am going through but some really don't my mom disappeared she was taken by a monster not by God.

Another thing, losing a loved one absolutely messes with them forever in some way. It flips everything you know upside down and yet you (I) are the ones left behind picking up those pieces to try to move forward. This has sent me on a whole different kind of roller coaster of emotions that I myself can't barely handle.

There is so many things I didn't prepare myself for. How could I how could anyone prepare themselves for something like this? Nothing no one could do to help or anything anyone could try to explain to me would help me feel at ease. This journey of grief is the most hardest things I have ever had to imagine that I would go through and everyday gets harder, even on the days that seem a little easier.

If I could tell my mom anything right now it would be to

tell her how much I love her and miss her so much and that I am so sorry I wasn't there when she needed me if only I would have been there maybe she would still be here I just want her back.

I want the world to know that if anyone out there knows anything about my mom's disappearance please let someone know. If you're not comfortable calling the police, you can go to my mom's Facebook page "In memory of Pamela Dunn" and leave a message, and I or someone will contact you. Someone out there knows something. So please, again, or just imagine it being someone you love, what would you do? How far would you go to find answers?

The community knew my mom. They knew she had a big heart her passion of helping people, her friendship, always making people laugh. She was an amazing woman that didn't deserve to be taken from her family and friends that love her so much she didn't deserve what happened to her. No one deserves that.

My mom's dreams were to watch her grandkids graduate and watch her daughter get married, and to move where there was mountains, and to be happy and in love with someone that would accept her and her kids and grand children. My dreams for my mom was just for her to be happy and to find that true love us women all want, to find that right man that would treat her like a princess, cause she deserved that. All she wanted was to be happy and he wouldn't allow that. He made sure if she wasn't happy with him then she wasn't gonna be happy with anyone else.

My mom was funny, always talking in her one voice that made u laugh so hard you were crying and laughing at the same time. My mom enjoyed having some time to enjoy being around friends and family playing darts and dancing.

She was always making sure she had her hair done and her makeup done before she would go places.

I followed her in those foot steps. I'm the same way even when her and I would take our drive around the lake turning up the music and jamming out to country music Shania Twain "Man I Feel like a Woman" was the name of the song lol. She was so much fun.

I never thought I would grow up with out her. It's been really hard on me and my kids. I lost a big part of me since she's been gone. I'm not the same fun, happy, energetic person I used to be, and I feel horrible that I can't be who I used to be for my kids. I wish I could; I just don't know how to get that person back or even if it's possible.

Stacey Bensen Thennis

Hi - My name is Mackenzie Benson. I am Pam Dunn's 1st grandchild.

My best memory with my grandma is she would make Mickey Mouse pancakes every morning. And she would let me help with dishes. When I got in trouble, she would spoil me rotten so I felt better. She loved working at Jenkins she would take residents to the zoo and to the park.

Her disappearance has caused a lot of issues mentally. I got diagnosed with PTSD and depression and anxiety. I have night terrors a lot ever since that happened.

If I could talk to her right now I would have her meet her great granddaughter and that I hope she is proud of me.

I want the world to know she was the most amazing and sweetest person in the world, and anyone that knew her would say the same thing.

The town of Watertown lost a good worker and an amazing person to talk to.

I miss everything about her she was my role model I hope she is proud of me still.

*Photo courtesy of Stacey Benson Thennis

Kelly Robinson
Unsolved Death

Memorial Day weekend, 1984, Kelly Robinson, 22, called her sister, Kathy, wanting to chat. Kathy, who was outside working at the time, instructed her little brother to tell Kelly she'd call her back.

That Saturday evening, Kelly, a vivacious, pretty girl with big, blue eyes, had gone out with friends to the Frontier Bar in Sioux Falls, and Kathy never had the chance to connect with her.

On Monday, Memorial Day, a family picnicking at a gravel-pit, pond 1.5 miles northeast of Luverne, MN, found a body floating in the frigid water. It was Kelly Robinson.

Kelly was wearing a jacket that had belonged to her recently deceased mother, and no clothing beneath her jeans. Detectives on the scene said she had defensive wounds on her hands, and it appeared she'd been asphyxiated.

Witnesses at the Frontier Bar saw her get into a vehicle that Saturday evening, but investigators are not sure how reliable those witnesses are.

Kelly had recently been through several traumatizing events in her life. One bright spot, her baby boy born in January of 1980, might have made all the difference had she later not been dealt the devastating diagnosis of Multiple Sclerosis. After struggling to navigate this debilitating disease, she made the painful decision to give her baby up for adoption. Kelly and her boyfriend moved to Rapid City to start fresh, but her disease escalated, forcing her into the hospital for several weeks. She eventually moved back to Sioux Falls. Then, in another blow, Kelly's mother died.

It began a downward spiral for Kelly, previously upbeat,

cheerful, artistic, outgoing, and happy, who then became withdrawn, quiet, and reserved.

To add to Kelly's ordeal, her diagnosis meant she could not drive and she had to depend on others for transportation.

Kelly found solace in socializing, and often frequented the Frontier Bar to hang out with friends. Her sister Kathy never imagined Kelly for much of a drinker, and in fact, when Kelly's body was found, there was no alcohol or drugs in her system.

Kelly Robinson had no connections to Luverne, MN, or anyone in that area. The location where her body was found just adds to the mystery of her death.

For your consideration:

~ Did Kelly's killer live in the Luverne, MN, area?

~ What made those tips or witnesses unreliable? Did they all describe something different?

~ Regardless of the reliability of the witnesses who saw her get into a car with someone, what became of those leads? Did authorities ever have a suspect?

~ Who was Kelly hanging out with that night at the Frontier bar? Did the other patrons recognize him or her? Or did she leave with someone who never entered the bar but picked her up outside?

~ Is there still evidence on file? Can it be tested for DNA or other forensic evidence?

If you know anything about the murder of Kelly Robinson, please contact

The MN BCA Tip Line at (877) 996-6222

Or to submit an anonymous tip, Minnesota CrimeStoppers at (800) 222-8477

Or submit an anonymous tip in SD, South Dakota CrimeStoppers at (605) 367-7007.

(Ref: MN BCA; *Argus Leader*; Kathy Moller)

I first met Kelly in my early years at Beresford High School. We became friends fast. She had that outgoing personality that you could see in the way she talked to you and laughed with you.

Trying to remember the things we did all these years later is a test of our minds. There was a group of us that hung out together. The memories we made are gems and conversation all these later.

The most certain memories I will always have is Kelly's ability to make you smile and feel at ease. Kelly was more of a people pleaser, was friends with everyone whether she knew you or not. You could say that she was a happy-go-lucky girl.

She lived with her mom in a small house on the edge of town (at the time). Her mom worked at Truck Towne Café' as a cook and took on extra shifts when she could. She wasn't there much when we were there with Kelly.

Through high school, we had a lot of fun whatever we did, like most teenagers. It was so much different back then. We were given free reign of the town, and parents never questioned us. So, of course, we took advantage of it. Pranks were our favorite thing to do, all for a laugh. We would push each other into the fountain in the middle of the Empire Mall in Sioux Falls, play hide and seek in the clothes racks, walk funny, and talk funny. Anything for a laugh or two.

I can honestly say that I only seen her upset a couple times, over boy problems, like all teenagers.

After graduation, we kept in contact quite often. I started at Stewart's School of Hairstyling the September after graduation, and she had a job and a small apartment close to where I lived. By then, she was expecting a baby, which she was very happy and excited about. Then when her son came, she was so proud of him and happy.

Then she became torn when she was trying to juggle work and home, and making sure her son had everything. He was very important to her. She wanted to be the best mom ever, and wanted her son to have a great life. I would go visit her, and we had long talks on how good she was, and what a great mom. But after awhile, she gave in and put him up for adoption, knowing he would have a better home, better life, and family surroundings. She wasn't a selfish person but knew this is what needed to be done. She knew she could see him again one day when she had her life on track.

That's when I lost touch with her, because of different schedules. I moved back to Beresford after that, and wasn't that close to her anymore.

When I heard the news of her death, I was devastated. Devastated over the loss of a great friend. If you met her and knew her, you would know why. She isn't one to forget easily. Her spunk and her energy are what I remember the best. That's what hurts the most, is trying to figure out how anyone could hurt her—a happy-go-lucky woman—and think that it was okay to take her life away. Away from family, friends, and the friends she never got to meet.

She will always live in our hearts and memories. When we, high school friends, get together for reunions, we think back at those fun days, and her name always comes up. Closure would be a great gift. We just want to know why??

Carla Zeimetz

I met Kelly Jean Robinson while growing up in Beresford, SD. She was a good friend of mine in High School. She was in my younger sister's class so she and her classmates and I hung out together.

Kelly had a zest for life and for having as much fun as she could. She was always trying to do something fun and to entertain her friends and make us laugh. She was the first one to take a dare. She never chickened out.

One time we went to Sioux Falls to go to the circus. We went to the pet store and picked up a bag of goldfish to take with us. We had talked Kelly into going to the concession stand and putting the fish into a cup of pop and watching who would buy it and of course, she did it. The pop was poured ahead of time, and she plopped the fish into the closet cup, sure enough, a man came right up and bought the cup of pop. Kelly watched where he went and followed him back to his seat. She approached him and asked if she could buy his pop. He, of course, was confused so she broke down and had to tell him what she did. We all got a good laugh out of it.

She loved her family so much. I remember her arguing with her mother one minute, her mom getting upset with her, and somehow she would manage to get her mom to laugh and break down to get what she wanted. She was a good big sister and aunt and she babysat her niece and nephew a lot.

Kelly was engaged once but never got married. She had asked me to be her Maid of Honor. We went wedding dress shopping and she picked out a beautiful dress. Not long after that, they called off the wedding. It was a good a thing because she was so young, but it was also a sad time for her.

I never got to see my friend get married but she would have made a wonderful wife because that girl loved deeply. I never got to see my friend raise a family, but I know that *she would have been the best mom that she could have been, because she always liked taking care of others.*

Kelly was very neat and took pride in dressing nicely. She was a great artist and I think that if she was alive today that she would have been some type of artist or beautician because she had a real gift in both areas.

Kelly made the world a better place. She had a great passion for life that she shared others.

I miss my friend, but I carry her memories deep in my heart and have never let her go. When I think of her, I get a big smile on my face, and let out a little laugh.

With Love,
Linda Merrick

If your loved one's case is not in this book and you would like to see it included in a possible second book, please contact me through my website at www.christinemagerwevik.com

Pah Pow
Missing Person

On Friday, April 15, 2016, Pah Pow, a petite Taiwanese woman, went out with her friends to a bar in Aberdeen for a couple drinks after work. They stated that she said she was leaving, telling them she was "good" to go home. The last physical evidence of Pah Pow is security camera footage of her leaving the bar, Zoo Bar, that night.

Pah Pow's husband, Sah Doe, claims that he last saw Pah Pow at their home in the 1000 block of 7th Avenue south of Aberdeen on April 17th, before he took their one-year-old child to the park. When he arrived back at home, she was gone. Their 10-year-old son, Lar Lar Say, said his mother had left in a vehicle with a man he recognized, but whose name he didn't know. Pow failed to arrive for her shift at DemKota Beef Plant on Monday and hasn't been seen since.

Due to a miscommunication, Pah Pow was not reported missing for a few days after she was last seen. Her family thought she was with friends, and her friends thought she was with family. It was also not unlike her to disappear for a couple days at a time and return home later.

Pah Pow left behind all of her personal possessions but had her phone, though it had been turned off after her disappearance.

Pah Pow's husband told authorities that they had been arguing shortly before her disappearance and that she had begun a relationship with another man after starting work at the beef plant. She had also blocked her husband from communicating with her over Facebook, which also added to their quarrels.

Through investigation, police found that Pah Pow was

not with her boyfriend.

Pah Pow and her husband shared four children, and had moved to Aberdeen, SD, from Lincoln, NE, after emigrating to the U.S. from Thailand. A few months after Pah Pow went missing, Sah Doe moved back to Nebraska with their children to be near his family. Pah Pow has family in the Omaha, NE, area, and they have said she hasn't been in contact with them since her disappearance.

Pah was 30 when she disappeared, is 5'2" and approximately 110 pounds. She has black hair, brown eyes, and has a history of seizures that tend to happen when she is upset. She speaks limited English, speaking mainly Karen and Thai. She was last seen wearing a white shirt, blue jeans, pink sneakers, a silver ring, and a silver necklace with a silver heart.

For your consideration:
~ Was Pah Pow a victim of stranger abduction?
~ Might the 10-year-old son be mistaken about the day he saw his mother get into a car with a familiar person?
~ Why would Pah Pow leave home without anything other than her phone?
~ Did Pah Pow decide to run away, turning off her phone so she could not be tracked?
~ Were there neighbors who may have seen her leave her home? Or was she actually last seen on Friday night after leaving the bar?

If you know anything about the disappearance of Pah Pow, please contact the
Aberdeen Police Department at (605) 626-7000

Or Brown County Sheriff's Department at (605) 626-7100
Or to submit an anonymous tip, contact Aberdeen CrimeStoppers at (605) 626-3500

(Ref: *KELOLAND News; Argus Leader; Aberdeen News;* The Charley Project)

Katrina Wind
Unsolved Death

On New Year's Eve, 1985, 21-year-old Katrina Wind, her sister, and a friend were out celebrating in Aberdeen, SD, when Katrina's sister and the friend decided they were done and going home. Katrina wanted to continue the celebration.

Later that night, around 1-2 a.m. on January 1st, 1986, Katrina returned home, but wanted to go out again. Her sister begged her not to, but Katrina left on foot.

Katrina's sister had contacted authorities earlier in the evening, concerned about Katrina's well being. She also contacted them again after Katrina left for the second time.

At 5:17 a.m. on that morning, law enforcement agencies were informed of a fatal hit-and-run one half mile south of the truck stop at the intersection of U.S. Highway 12 and SD Highway 281 in Aberdeen. It was Katrina Wind.

When the call about the fatal hit-and-run came in, according to an article published in the American News, provided to *KELOLAND News* by the Aberdeen Library, Police Sgt. Bill Rappe stated that he had given a young woman a ride to the Park Village Mobile Home Court near the Starlite Cafe. He feared it was the same woman. When they arrived on the scene, his fears were confirmed.

Ambulance services received a call around 5:21 a.m. When they arrived, they found Katrina Wind dead. Through subsequent investigation by multiple law enforcement agencies, they found she had been struck by one vehicle, killing her, and then by a second vehicle. The couple in the second vehicle had contacted Aberdeen police through the Starlite Cafe.

When Katrina's sister contacted authorities earlier about Katrina, she was told that an officer had picked her up and dropped her off at home. But Katrina never arrived home. She learned later that the officer had dropped Katrina off at a trailer where she did not live.

There are conflicting reports regarding the details about when the officer dropped Katrina off at the mobile home. In one news report, it states that the officer claimed Katrina never went to the door of the trailer. But in the KELOLAND News article, Katrina's sister states that she was told by the officer that Katrina went in to the mobile home, but didn't know anyone there.

Family members wonder if something happened to Katrina at the mobile home she was dropped off at, but officers in charge of the investigation state in the *KELOLAND News* article that the snow on the ground gave them "a 'pristine' pallet for law enforcement to trace Wind's path." It goes on to state that they said, "We followed her tracks back to the north. She was walking back and forth, meandering (into the highway). She had walked roughly half a mile." (Quote by Officer Phil Toft.)

No autopsy was performed on Katrina Wind, but family members believe an autopsy may have provided other details about how Katrina died. Katrina's sister stated that she thought Katrina may have been shot. She said, "There was a one-inch gash on her forehead and an eyelid was torn."

Katrina left behind a 4-year-old daughter.

For your consideration:
~ Why was Katrina confused about where the officer could drop her off?

~ Did the officer see Katrina go into the mobile home or not?

~ Why was an autopsy not done? Can an autopsy still be done, if the family chooses?

~ Is there still evidence that might provide more details in the way of advanced forensic testing?

If you know anything about the hit-and-run death of Katrina Wind, please contact
The South Dakota Highway Patrol at (605) 773-3105
Or Aberdeen Police Department at (605) 626-7000
Or Brown County Sheriff's Department at (605) 626-7100
Or submit an anonymous tip at (605) 626-3500.

(Ref: *KELOLAND News; Aberdeen News; American News;* Belinda Joe)

Morgan Lewis
Unsolved Death
Closed Without Closure

While I hesitate to cover cases that are considered closed by law enforcement, there are a few that leave far too many lingering questions to discount. This is one of those cases.

Shortly before 6 a.m. on the morning of November 1, 2004, a custodian by the name of Roger Hoffman discovered a body on the campus grounds outside the west entrance of Seymour Hall at Northern State University in Aberdeen, SD. The body was that of 46-year-old Morgan Lewis, a new German professor at the college. He'd been shot in the back of the neck, on the left side.

Morgan Lewis had moved from California and had been a professor at NSU for only about two and a half months at the time of his death. His partner, James Buck, stayed in California, waiting to hear from Morgan about whether Aberdeen and NSU was a good fit.

When the autopsy was done, the pathologist stated that it didn't appear that Lewis committed suicide. The initial death certificate listed homicide as the manner of death, and stated that Lewis died of a single gunshot wound to the neck with a .25 caliber handgun. The wound, according to Pathologist Brad Randall, was a "very close-range shot to the neck...a bit short of contact, but very close-range wound to the neck."

Upon further investigation, officers discovered a .25 caliber Colt handgun in the dumpster 40 feet away. No prints were found on the gun.

After over a year of investigation, a huge shake up in the

police department, and consultation by outside sources, the manner of death was changed to suicide. The case was considered closed, and by multiple accounts, the police are under no obligation to disclose details about the case or how they arrived at their conclusion. Yet, details seem to have emerged that are not verified in all media sources found online.

The aforementioned details of this case are fairly well documented. But from here forward, details about this case are murky, depending on the multiple sources found on his death.

According to an article published by the *Aberdeen News*, there was a puddle of blood near, or leading to or away from the dumpster where the gun was found. Other sources—online, and including people I've spoken to who were there that day—state there was no blood near, or leading to or away from the dumpster.

The *Aberdeen News* article also included an excerpt from an earlier publication, in November of 2004, that an "anonymous police source said that one person of interest was questioned in Lewis' death, but no charges were filed in the death that authorities had yet to classify." (This information is only in question because of the anonymous source.) It goes on to state that "Brown County Coroner Kevin Spitzer said that because of the circumstances surrounding the death, he listed homicide as the manner of death. He was quoted as saying, 'There was a gunshot wound. The death certificate can always be amended if it turns out it wasn't a homicide, but that's what seemed most likely,' and that instead of homicide he could have marked suicide or pending, but he chose not to. Brad Randall, forensic pathologist, stated in the later publication of

Aberdeen News that "Sometimes coroners do that just to make sure cases get investigated."

One article found online states that Morgan was found only in his t-shirt and slacks, and that his jacket, keys, and backpack were found inside the building, in his office. It also states that his wallet was found near his body, empty. And yet another source stated that the gun was found underneath trash in the dumpster, apparently hidden.

According to an article in the *Rapid City Journal* from December of 2004, information not found elsewhere in any online articles, an affidavit states, "These circumstances would suggest that Lewis had been shot by someone. The document states, 'A blood trail ran from Lewis' body to an area near a dumpster about 40 yards away.' And "it also says an empty shell casing was found near the garbage can." Being quoted as an "affidavit," this would imply that it was a written statement made under oath. However, while affidavits are admissible as evidence, some courts may consider it hearsay document, and not admissible.

There is little mention of the weapon, only that it was a .25 caliber Colt handgun, and nothing about who the gun was registered to, or if authorities had that information.

Also mentioned in one of the online articles: throughout the 18-month investigation, investigators apparently discovered a story written by Morgan Lewis about a professor who commits suicide, which may have helped authorities reach the conclusion that this was suicide.

In one article that discussed details of the case (which were not found elsewhere online), evidence of gunpowder residue was found on both of Morgan's hands, and blowback (blood, tissue, etc) was found on the gun and his left hand, which would indicate that Morgan had been holding or had contact with or was very near the gun that killed him. Not that it rules anything out, but it should be noted that Morgan was right-handed.

By all accounts both online and personal, Morgan was cheerful, involved, and well liked by students and co-workers on campus. Most agree that he was possibly stressed, taking on a lot of extra projects, such as teaching at Hutterville Colony School through DDN technology and three hours a day at Aberdeen Central High School, working on independent study projects for several students and occasionally tutoring Native American students at NSU.

Morgan was fluent in English, German, French, and Spanish, and held a doctorate in German with Specialization in Pedegogy (Second Language Acquisition) from the University of California.

Later news reports state that James Buck, Morgan's partner of 20 years, filed suit against Prudential Insurance Company in Federal Court for $150,000 in death benefits that were denied because Aberdeen police ruled the death of Morgan Lewis as suicide. While Prudential maintains that the death was suicide and therefore Buck was not entitled to the payout, their company's medical director determined that the gunshot wound on the back and left side of Lewis' neck was not consistent with suicide because Lewis was right-handed. A settlement was reached out of court.

Public opinion seems to be split about down the middle as to whether Dr. Lewis was murdered or committed suicide. I offer these questions as a basis for conversation, not as an argument to convince you of one or the other.

For your consideration:

~ Why, if he was so stressed, was he involved in so many projects? Was he unable to say no, or were they given to him without concern for his wellbeing? Or were those activities his outlet?

~ If, indeed, those extra projects caused him to be stressed, possibly suicidal, why would he not just quit and go back to California, rather than commit suicide?

~ Why are there conflicting reports about a blood trail between the body and the dumpster where the gun was found? Who do we believe? People who saw the crime scene that day, or those who report what they were told?

~ What, if any, did Morgan's case have to do with the inner turmoil of the Aberdeen Police Department happening about the same time as the investigation?

~ If Morgan wanted to commit suicide, but make it look like murder:

    1. How could he count on shooting himself in the neck, and survive long enough to wipe prints from the gun, put it in the dumpster, and die elsewhere, away from the dumpster?

    2. And if he were going to be successful in making it look like a murder, wouldn't he have picked up the (alleged) spent shell casing, and put it in the dumpster as well? Or shot himself on the sidewalk or near the door to ensure the shell casing was near his body, then thrown the gun away in the dumpster, and returned to the spot near the building before dying?

    3. Why would he make it appear as though he came outside after arriving in the building? Why not leave his jacket on, and have all of his belongings on him when he shot himself? Why complicate and confuse things, by

putting his belongings inside and just wearing a t-shirt outside the building? Wouldn't he want it to appear as though he were jumped, maybe robbed, right outside the building as he was arriving for work, completely dressed with his backpack, keys, etc?

4. Yes, a right-handed person, trying to stage a suicide to look like murder, might use their left hand to shoot themself. But imagine this: You're trying to shoot yourself in the neck, not hit the spine so you don't drop where you are, do just enough damage to fatally injure yourself but not die instantly, and yet you must hold the gun at just the right angle with your non-dominant hand. (Remember the coroner stated the gun was close but not touching the skin.) How easy would this be? How do you assure the exact placement and trajectory to accomplish such specific goals? Wouldn't it have been easier if the gun was touching the skin, somewhat held in place?

5. How difficult would it be for a right-handed person to shoot themselves on the back, left side of their neck, especially if they wanted to survive long enough to stage the scene?

6. Dr. Lewis was highly educated. If he planned a suicide, staged to look like murder, emptying his wallet beforehand, planning the planting of the gun after shooting himself, wiping away fingerprints from the gun, moving away from the dumpster, all the details involved in making this look like murder, how could he be so careless and sloppy as to leave a story about a professor committing suicide on his computer for investigators to find?

7. What motive would Morgan Lewis have to stage a suicide to look like murder? For the insurance policies? If a person was truly depressed enough to commit suicide,

would they care so much about making sure their partner was able to claim life insurance payouts?

8. Does the gunpowder residue and blowback evidence exclude the possibility of murder? Could Morgan have been trying to fend off the gunshot, thereby getting both gunpowder and blowback on his hands?

9. Would Morgan take that chance that he might not die, but be merely wounded, disfigured, or worse, end up a quadriplegic, or in a vegetative state?

10. Wouldn't someone who was going to shoot themselves and make it look like murder and *not* want to leave a blood trail from the dumpster where they threw the gun, think to shoot themselves in an area of their body that wouldn't bleed profusely, like the stomach or someplace on the body where they could contain the blood until they reached an area away from that dumpster? Wouldn't they want to *avoid* leaving a blood trail?

~ If this was, in fact, a murder:

1. With gunpowder residue found on Morgan's hands, how would it have gotten there, and if placed by the killer, why?

2. What possible reason would a killer have to put a gun in a dumpster near the body? Why not take it with them?

3. What motive would a killer have to take Morgan's life? Was it robbery? Was it personal?

4. Could Morgan's possible murder be racially motivated, as he was part Native American? Could it have been motivated by homophobia?

5. Whose gun was it? Are there no serial numbers or registrations linking the gun to anyone?

~ 18 months earlier, on May 3rd, 2003, 20-year-old Tyler

O'Neil, was found dead in the lobby of Jerde Hall on the NSU campus. A sophomore at NSU was originally charged with manslaughter and assault, but the charges were later dropped because of a lack of evidence. Is it possible that, as some in the community suspect, the suicide ruling of Morgan's death was somewhat influenced by the university's wish not to further harm their image with two unexplained deaths?

If you know anything about the death of Dr. Morgan Lewis, please contact the
Aberdeen Police Department at (605) 626-7000
Or Brown County Sheriff's Office at (605) 626-7100
Or submit an anonymous tip at (605) 626-3500 (Aberdeen CrimeStoppers).

(Ref: *Aberdeen News; Rapid City Journal; The Dickenson Press; Victoria Advocate; South Dakota Politics; Argus Leader,* James Buck)

Morgan Lewis

Morgan Nevin Lewis was born on April 12, 195,8 in Fresno, California, at Saint Agnes Hospital. His mother was Jane Margaret Lewis and she was born in Iowa City, Iowa, on August 6, 1919. Her maiden name was Nevin. She died in Sonora, California on February 11, 1990. His father was William Francis Lewis, and he was born in Gregory South Dakota on January 10, 1914. He married Jane Margaret Nevin on December 31, 1945 in San Bernardino, California. He died on March 23, 1980 at the family home in Tuolumne County, California. Morgan's maternal Grandfather was John Lewis Nevin and he was the head of Saint Bernadine's Hospital, in San Bernardino California, where I was born in 1948. Morgan had one sister, and her name is Jane and currently lives in Tuolumne, California.

Morgan studied language from an early age. He studied French at Institut Francile Canoe Island Camps, Inc in August 1973 when he was 15 years old. It was an 8-week course. The course was taught on an island off of the coast of Washington

State. His love of language had begun. He studied German in 1975 by living in Germany and participating in the AFS program. He lived with a family and stayed in touch with them until his death in 2004.

In March 1984, Morgan earned two Bachelor of Arts degrees from the University of California at Irvine. One degree was for a major in drama and one degree was for a major in German.

I met Morgan on Labor Day 1984 at the swimming pool of the housing complex in which we lived. Because of shyness on my part, it took about 3 hours before I had enough courage to speak to him. We formed a relationship and lived together as partners from December 1984 until his death in 2004. A little bit over 20 years. It took me 3 months to come to terms with the 10-year age difference.

In December 1988, Morgan earned a Master of Arts degree in German from the University of Southern California, and then in only an additional three years, a Doctor of Philosophy degree, also in German, and also from the University of Southern California. He earned his PHD faster than any student in the department up until that time. In March of 1992, Morgan received the Center for Excellence in Teaching Award for Outstanding Departmental Teaching Assistant in the German Department at the University of Southern California. While he was proud of these achievements, he requested that the title of Doctor not be used when referencing him, and he requested that the name over his office door at Northern State University read Morgan Lewis.

I can't say that Morgan had a favorite subject. He liked them all. I called him a professional student. The final classes he took were with me at the Massage School of Santa Monica. We both loved learning about muscles in the body and enjoyed helping people that were in need of muscle pain relief. It was a 150-hour, three month course.

Hobbies and interests for Morgan were varied. We traveled many times to Europe either by air or cruise ship, and enjoyed visiting the Baltic area, including St. Petersburg, and all the way to the top of the world in Norway. We enjoyed Paris and our stay at the George V hotel, the Eurostar Chunnel crossing under the English Channel, England and Scotland and Morgan had a great time in Germany. We sailed through the Panama Canal and down the West Coast between Vancouver and Los Angeles. We visited Maui and Oahu more times than we could count and planned to spend our final years together on Maui. Morgan's ashes are scattered in a quiet bay overlooking the Southern coast of Maui. We spent time in Alaska, either cruising through the Inside Passage or fishing for salmon with friends on the Kenai Peninsula or deep-sea fishing for halibut off the Alaskan coast.

I never saw Morgan without knowing there was a book close by. When he was at home and not teaching, he was at the library at least once a week. The library staff used to ask him if the book they were planning to read was any good. He had probably read it. He subscribed to People magazine in Spanish, just to keep his Spanish current and alive. He read popular novels in German and French for the same reason.

He returned to South Dakota because Northern State University offered him a teaching position. He was looking forward to being there, but sad that we would be apart for such long periods. He got a cell phone with X amount of free minutes, so we talked on the phone at least twice a day and more on the weekends.

Morgan's life was about contribution. Though he was very private, he could reach out to people and make a difference in their days and their lives. I never met anyone that knew him that didn't like him and want to spend more time in his presence. I was just lucky that he chose me to share his life.

Some random thoughts I have about Morgan Lewis:

He would make up happy songs and sing them all day long. He would sing them to me even though he couldn't carry a tune.

He did not talk to dogs. He grew up with at least a dozen dogs and cats. His favorite was a little dog named Whitey.

He could tell you the month and year a popular song was released and played on the radio. He could also sing most of the lyrics

He could say the lines of dialogue of most of the cast of the "I love Lucy" TV series before the character would say them.

He liked to sing "Lily of the Valley" from "I love Lucy". It was a song Ethel sang.

If he put something on his plate, he ate it.

He liked every cookie I ever made.

He didn't like to cook, do housework, or yard work. But, he did all of them fairly well when he had to.

He had social skills for any occasion.

He didn't use bad words. I heard two come out of his mouth in 20 years. He didn't care for pornography at all.

He drank red wine or Scotch as a rule. He never tried recreational drugs or marijuana.

He had big blue eyes and a bigger smile that will be remembered forever. Just ask anyone that met him.

I still think of him daily.

James Buck

*Photo courtesy of James Buck

In the few months that he had been at NSU, Morgan Lewis played a part in an amazing number of lives: sometimes a small role, at other times a rather large role.

Morgan was a special blessing to me. Since Morgan was teaching at Aberdeen Central and in our e-learning center, he was applying for SD teacher certification. Although Lakota was his first language and though he had taught college-level courses in Plains Indian history and culture, that wasn't good enough for DECA: he was going to have to take INED 411, South Dakota Native Americans. Making the situation more ironic, is that, when Dr. Neville was called up to active duty, I ended up teaching the course, and so Morgan was going to have to take the course from me! After talking with him and realizing that he knew far, far more about the subject than I did, Morgan and I agreed that, instead of just taking the class a regular student, he'd help me teach parts of the course.

Now I was only going to ask him for a class session or two, but sensing my need for help, Morgan ended up coming to every class. It was wonderful to have someone in the class who actually spoke Lakota, and who could answer many of the student questions about which I hadn't a clue. But more than that, I appreciated Morgan's constant encouragement. He'd always stay after class to talk and exchange ideas, never focusing on what hadn't gone well (though I'm sure he could have found many things to be critical of in my presentations), but concentrating on what was good. For the rest of the semester, there will be this huge gap...the place where Morgan should be, but isn't.

Most of you will probably have similar feelings. For Morgan's students, you'll be missing the man who should be at the front of the class, but isn't. For his colleagues, you'll maybe be missing the man who should be there in his third floor Seymour office but isn't, or the man who should be working with you on one project or another but isn't. "Oh for the touch of a vanished hand and the sound of a voice that is stilled," said Keats, and, even for those who knew Morgan only casually, there is something greatly disturbing in knowing that invariably friendly way he greeted everyone is gone, and we won't hear that voice on campus again.

Art Marmorstein, NSU professor

Kevin Duane Marshall
Missing Person

On Thursday, May 19, 2016, Kevin was at his mother Eleanor's home in Eagle Butte, SD, where they discussed plans to attend his daughter's high school graduation in Rapid City.

Eleanor Miner, Kevin's mother, stated that on Thursday, May 19, she told Kevin she was leaving Eagle Butte to go to Rapid City. Kevin told her he would be going to his daughter's graduation but did not want to ride with Eleanor. She told him she would be back on Friday, and she would take him to Rapid City on Saturday. She last saw him on Thursday.

Friday morning, May 20th, he spoke with his sister at Eleanor's house and asked his sister if she was going to Rapid City. She said no. He then told her he was leaving to go to Rapid City. He didn't have a car, so he was going to walk the 270 miles to reach Rapid City by Sunday, the day of her graduation ceremony. He walked out the door and was never seen again.

Family members claim that, although Kevin had issues with drugs and alcohol, he would never miss his daughter's graduation. He cared about his daughters and was so proud that his oldest child was about to graduate.

Though rumors circulate constantly about where he might be found, who might have had reason to hurt him, nothing ever materialized. There has been no trace of him, no belongings, no evidence, nothing.

Kevin was born May 4, 1978, and was 38-years-old when he went missing. He is approximately 5'11" and 165-190 pounds, with short, black hair and brown eyes. He has a

1.5" scar on top of his head, a circular-shaped birthmark on his left elbow. In 2011, Kevin had a broken jaw/fractured chin, and may have a metal plate or pin in it.

Kevin has several tattoos. On his right forearm is the word "Jewett." On his left arm are the initials "CH" and a skull with a joker hat, and on his left forearm are the initials "KDM." On his neck is the tattoo of a medicine wheel (a circle with a cross in the center), but this tattoo has been filled in to make a larger, unknown tattoo.

For your consideration:
~ Was Kevin the victim of a hit-and-run, and the perpetrators hid his body? Is Kevin a victim of an accident or murder?
~ Could Kevin have simply left town to start a new life? As important as his girls were to him, how would he have been able to stay hidden for so many years?
~ Did Kevin get into a vehicle with someone who eventually harmed or killed him and dumped him somewhere or buried him?
~ What, if any, leads do law enforcement officials have on his case? Is there more to be done?
~ Did Kevin actually make it out of Eagle Butte? Is there a chance that he left the house and tried to find a ride from someone in town?

If you know anything about the disappearance of Kevin Duane Marshall, please contact the Cheyenne River Sioux Tribal Police at (605) 964-4567

Or submit an anonymous tip at (605) 218-0014.

(Ref: *Native Sun News Today;* The Charley Project; Eleanor Miner)

My son, Kevin, was a determined man. He knew it was 278 miles to Rapid City, and was going to do whatever he needed to do to get to his daughter's graduation. That was his oldest child graduating, and he was pretty excited about it.

He was a good man. His kids were pretty important to him. He's got three girls and he was so proud of his girls. He'd travel back and forth between Eagle Butte and Rapid City, but he would always call me to let me know where he was. He wasn't that kind to disappear; he'd be gone, but it never failed, he'd call me. Or he'd show up. He'd wait at my house until I got off work.

He always made it a point to let me know how he was doing, or what he was doing, he didn't want me to be stressed out. Then no calls. No nothing. All three of his girls graduated, and no letters, no calls… And those were important things for him. He couldn't believe his oldest daughter was actually graduating. He was just all excited. It's so odd that he would just disappear like that without a trace.

He was pretty close to his girls, and their mother and him were separated, but he'd kept in touch for his girls. He loved them with all his heart.

I lost my grandson, then Kevin disappeared, then I lost another son, and now Kevin's daughter. It's been a rough seven years.

Eleanor Miner

*Photo courtesy of Eleanor Miner

If your loved one's case is not in this book and you would like to see it included in a possible second book, please contact me through my website at www.christinemagerwevik.com

Pamela Halverson
Unsolved Death

On Tuesday, August 3 1999, Barb Ewoldt knew something was seriously wrong when her daughter's employer, Citibank's Family Center, called to say that Pamela, 27, hadn't shown up for work. Her father reported her missing that afternoon.

Two days later, at about 8:45 on Thursday morning, Pamela's car was found several blocks from her residence, in the 2800 block of East 11th Street in Sioux Falls, SD. Her body was in the back seat of her car.

Pamela's mother stated that Pamela had been strangled, and that her car was found behind The Pocket Lounge near the volleyball sand pit. The owner of the lounge told authorities that he hadn't noticed Pamela's car there, and that it wasn't uncommon for cars to be left for a day or two, as many patrons would leave their vehicles if they'd had too much to drink.

Her mother stated in an article that although she was devastated, she wasn't terribly surprised. Pamela, the mother of a 9-year-old son, had been in a tumultuous relationship with her live-in boyfriend, Gary Javers, and had two protective orders taken out against him, the first was dismissed. Pamela had the second protection order in her purse the day her body was discovered, but the purse was never found.

Pamela and Gary lived at 1806 S. Cleveland, and Pamela had been recently trying to get Gary Javers out of her home, filing a protection order against him. She later dismissed that order after he was arrested for beating her and busting the windows out of her car.

Police searched Pamela's and Gary's residence once the investigation into her death began. Gary told authorities that Pamela went to Wal-Mart and left her dog and son behind for him to watch.

Gary Javers, named as a "person of interest," professed his innocence in Pamela's death up until his passing in 2013.

Authorities would state in a *KELOLAND News* interview that they had a suspect but could not name him, and that they believed the suspect had passed away in 2013.

Pamela's parents went on to raise her son, Tylor.

Law enforcement officials believe it may still be possible to solve the case of Pamela's murder, and that advancements in forensic technology may help.

For your consideration:

~ Has the evidence in Pamela's case been reexamined and analyzed with more current, technologically advanced methods?

~ If the crime can be linked to someone who has passed away, is there motivation to close this case? Whose motivation?

~ Can something be done about the ostensible futility of protection orders? Is there some way to make them more effective? Or do we need to overhaul this flaw in the system?

If you know anything about the murder of Pamela Halverson, please contact the

Sioux Falls Police Department at (605) 367-7234

Or submit an anonymous tip to Sioux Falls CrimeStoppers at (605) 367-7007

(Ref: *Argus Leader; KELOLAND News; Dakota News Now; Barb Ewoldt*)

My daughter, Pam, was born Pamela Ann East. She had two younger brothers, Matthew and Mark. She was a very quiet child, never any problems whatsoever. Throughout her life, she loved school, and really enjoyed animals, and when she got older, children became very important to her.

She married Kris Halverson in 1989, and in 1990, she gave birth to her son, Tylor. Kris and Pamela divorced when Tylor was one year old. He was the center of her life, and she doted on him. Because she was a young parent, and she enjoyed him so much, they did a lot of "kid stuff" together—games, bouncy houses, bicycle riding, things of that nature.

She had various jobs, and she and I both worked at Dairy Queen and Taco Johns, which could be lots of fun. In fact, she could just look at me and tell if I was stressed. She was very kind and very loving, and once when I was going through kind of a rough time, she brought me a rose to work, just to make me feel better.

As the kids got older, she and Matt and Mark, she became their advisor. She was the person they went to when they got older, when they needed to talk or needed help working through something. They got along very well, and they trusted her. Matt and Pam were only two years apart, so they were very close. And when Mark came along three and a half years later, he was her baby. She adored him.

When she passed, she was working at Citibank Daycare and she just loved that job because of her love for children. In fact, she'd even work on weekends watching some of those kids so their parents could go out.

She had a love of God, and a deep faith. We know that we will see her later.

Barb Trageser Ewoldt

Axel Christensen
Unsolved Death

On the evening of April 12th, 1984, Axel Christensen, a retired John Morrell employee, was found dead in his home. Reports state that his foster son, David, and his son-in-law went to check on him and found him shot to death in his basement. Axel's car was found a few blocks away.

Days later, his foster son, David Bear, 22, was arrested for accessory after the fact in the homicide, and for altering and destroying evidence that might lead to his foster father's killer. During Bear's arraignment, then-State's Attorney Jack Hanson read the charge against Bear, stating that Bear had "assisted another person in concealing, destroying or altering any physical evidence that might aid in the discovery, arrest, prosecution, or conviction of that other person." The other person was never named in the charge.

In early June of that year, divers dragged the Big Sioux River looking for evidence, but the officer in charge of the search declined to say what they were looking for.

David Bear was one of 59 foster children, along with four natural children, that Axel Christensen and his wife, Irene had raised throughout their married life. After Irene's passing, Bear lived with Axel in his home.

The trial, set to begin Nov 14th, 1984, ended with an acquittal of David Bear. The case is still unsolved.

For your consideration:
~ What motive would anyone have to kill Axel? Was anything missing that might indicate robbery?

~ No details are found stating what evidence law enforcement found. What evidence, if any, tied David to this murder?

~ Who was the unnamed person tied to David in this investigation? Why are they unnamed?

~ What evidence were divers looking for in the Big Sioux River?

If you know anything about the murder of Axel Christensen, please contact the
Sioux Falls Police Department at (605) 367-7212
Minnehaha County Sheriff's Office at (605) 367-4300
Or to submit an anonymous tip, contact CrimeStoppers at (877) 367-7007.

(Ref: *Argus Leader, June, 1984; Argus Leader, Sept, 1984*)

Donna Marie Larrabee
Missing Person

On November 17, 1976, Donna Marie Larrabee, 16, boarded a Greyhound bus in Rapid City, SD, headed to Sacramento, California, to see her father.

Donna Marie lived in Rapid City with her mother and relatives. But after leaving Rapid City, it is unclear if she ever made it to California. The bus route traveled through South Dakota, Wyoming, Utah, Nevada, and California. No trace of Donna Marie Larrabee has ever been found.

There are few details about her disappearance. Her father continued to search for her until his death, and now her brother has taken up the search for her.

Donna Marie was born June 7, 1960, and is Native American descent. At the time of Donna's disappearance, she was 5'6" tall and weighed 120 pounds, with black hair and brown eyes, and also wore glasses.

For your consideration:
~ Why was Donna traveling alone to California?
~ Was Donna running away or were prior arrangements made with her father?
~ What clues, if any, were uncovered at any of the stops along the route to California?

If you know anything about Donna's disappearance, please contact the
Rapid City Police Department at (605) 394-4133
Or Pennington County Sheriff's Department at (605) 394-6113
Or submit an anonymous tip, text RCPD and your info to 847411.

Photo courtesy of Randall Larrabee
(Ref: The Charley Project; The Doe Network; Justice for Native People)

Joleen Hass
Unsolved Death

On the afternoon of November 10, 1975, a Rapid City Police Department detective and a DCI special agent arrived at Rapid City's Delroy Motel on Sturgis Road to find the body of undercover narcotics agent Joleen Hass Schutte, 22. She'd been strangled and stabbed to death. Ms. Hass was a witness at an upcoming trial in a drug-related case.

Joleen Hass had moved to Rapid City from Sioux City, IA, where she began work as an undercover agent for the Iowa Bureau of Criminal Investigation, the Drug Enforcement Administration, and the Sioux City Police Department, while waiting tables as a cover. She then began work for the SD Attorney General's office in South Dakota's more metropolitan areas of Yankton, Vermillion, Spearfish, Sturgis, and finally, Rapid City for the RCPD and the Pennington County Sheriff's office. Joleen's father, well aware of her undercover work, was quoted in an article after her death, saying she'd been undercover for three years. Other sources claim she worked undercover for Des Moines, and yet others state she began in Sioux City. In any case, in the 20 months prior to her death, Joleen was responsible for the arrest and conviction of numerous offenders.

Authorities believe Joleen may have known her attacker, as there were no signs of forced entry into her room. They said she was likely struck on the head, dragged to the bed, strangled, then stabbed to death. Medical examinations show that she was stabbed a total of 12 times, twice directly to the heart. She had eaten shortly before her death, leading officials to wonder if she had been followed from the restaurant.

Agent Hass was set to testify in the drug trial of James Clark of North Sioux City, SD, when she was found dead. With Hass having previously testified against him in a preliminary hearing, Clark was convicted of those drug charges. While Clark was free on bond pending a South Dakota Supreme Court appeal of his conviction, he was murdered on August 8, 1977, by James Donald Cowell. Five weeks after his disappearance, Clark's body was found in a shallow grave on his farm near North Sioux City, SD. Cowell was later convicted in Clark's murder.

Authorities in SD and IA speculated that Clark had hired someone to kill Hass to prevent her from testifying, not knowing that she'd already supplied authorities with the information to convict him.

A month before her murder while working with law enforcement in Sturgis, Joleen was brutally assaulted. Two days later, she moved into the Delroy Motel in Rapid City. Her attack in Sturgis was never solved.

Immediately after her death, authorities purposely did not divulge that she was undercover, allowing articles of a salacious nature about her to circulate in the hopes that the perpetrator or perpetrators might brag about killing a snitch or informant, (knowing that no one would likely admit to or brag about killing a law enforcement agent, a capital felony.)

After Joleen's death, SD Governor Richard Kneip sent a letter to Joleen's parents, thanking them for their daughter's service. At Joleen's funeral, SD Attorney General William Janklow delivered the eulogy and presented her parents with a South Dakota flag as a memorial and a token of gratitude, telling them that Joleen had performed "above and beyond the call of" duty, and "made South Dakota a better place to live." Five Sioux City, IA, police officers and one South Dakota DEA agent served as Joleen's pallbearers.

For your consideration:
~ Did SD authorities do all they could to protect Joleen Hass? Then again, as an agent, did Hass need or request protection, or did she not sense she was in danger?
~ Did her attack in Sturgis have anything to do with her death in Rapid City?
~ Did Clark, in fact, hire someone to kill her?
~ Or was she killed by someone else, maybe someone she knew?

If you know anything about the murder of Agent Joleen Hass Schutte, please contact the Rapid City Police Department at (605) 394-4131
Or Pennington County Sheriff's Office at (605) 394-6113
Or DCI at (605) 394-1884
Or submit an anonymous tip text RCPD and your tip to 847411

(Ref: *Rapid City Journal; Sioux City Journal; Fort Dodge Messenger; Des Moines Register; Argus Leader*; Kathy Newcomb)

"Days will pass into years, but I will always remember you with silent tears." ~ Author unknown

My sister died as a result of trying to make this world a better place. She was my best friend growing up. We always did everything together – horseback riding, swimming, bike riding, walking downtown to O'Connell Drugstore to have a malt or banana split and just laugh, and talk about anything and everything.

I often wonder what it would have been like to go through life together. You left us way too soon but I know you are in a safe and much better place. You will be forever in my heart and someday we will be together again. I miss and love you!

Kathy

My dearest big sister. You left a huge void in our hearts and our family when you left this earth. I didn't get time to really know you but as we were becoming adults I feel like we would have been close friends and confidants. I miss you more than words can ever express. Till we meet in heaven RIP

Pam

Arnold Archambeau and Ruby Ann Bruguier
Unsolved Death
Closed Without Closure

Arnold "Picotte" Archambeau and Ruby Ann Bruguier, long-time sweethearts, were members of the Yankton Sioux Tribe and lived in Lake Andes, SD. Lake Andes is a small town, 1992 population of 850, in the Yankton Indian Reservation in southeast South Dakota. Arnold and Ruby, well liked in the community, met in high school and fell in love, and eventually had a baby, Erika Marie.

In one article, Ruby's father, Quentin, described Ruby as a gentle person, laughing and joking around. Arnold was popular, crowned prom king in high school. At the time of his disappearance, he worked at Fort Randall Casino.

On the blustery night of December 11, 1992, in Lake Andes, SD, Ruby, 19, made plans to have an all-night party, enjoying some free time. Ruby began partying at her apartment with her sister, Danita, and Yvonne and Tracy Dion, her cousins. After a while, they went to a bar called Runge's and stayed until it closed. Afterwards, they went to a party at a friend's house. Danita stayed at the party but Ruby and Tracy later met up with Arnold, 20, and went out driving around.

Around 6 a.m., Arnold, Ruby, and Tracy arrived at Tracy's parents, Charlie and Rita's house to pick up 16-month-old Erika. Charlie, seeing that they'd been drinking, suggested they go home and pick up Erika later in the day. They agreed and drove off in Arnold's Chevy Monte Carlo with Arnold at the wheel, Ruby in the front passenger seat, and Tracy in the back.

Just outside Lake Andes, on Highway 281, they reached an intersection, and Tracy claims that Arnold said there was no other cars in view, and wanted to "spin out." Within seconds, the car landed upside down in the frozen ditch. When Tracy got her bearings, she realized Arnold was not in the car. Ruby was in the front, hitting the dash and door, saying, "Oh, my God! Oh, my God!" Ruby continued struggling until she got the door open enough to squeeze out, but the door immediately closed before Tracy could escape.

A short time later, help arrived, and Tracy was rescued from the car. She told authorities that she last saw Arnold and Ruby walking away from the accident site with no visible signs of injury and didn't understand why they would abandon her.

Throughout that night, law enforcement searched for Arnold and Ruby. The ditch where the car landed was between the lake and the highway, and although it had water in it, it was frozen solid. Searchers scoured the area and out onto the lake, but found no trace of Arnold or Ruby or any holes in the ice where they could have fallen through. With very little snow, there were no footprints to follow. The accident occurred less than a mile away from town which made their disappearance even more puzzling.

Over the following days and weeks, multiple searches took place involving law enforcement, search teams, family members, and volunteers. While some suggested that Arnold and Ruby may have been laying low so they wouldn't be charged with DUI. Others, especially family, said that they would have at least called or found somewhere safe to hide out until they were sober, and that they wouldn't have stayed away longer than a day or two. It was also unusual that Arnold and Ruby would be gone that long without checking on baby Erika, particularly since Ruby was still breastfeeding the baby.

BODIES FOUND:

On March 10, 1993, three months after Arnold and Ruby disappeared, a man named Everdale Song Hawk of Lake Andes called the sheriff's office, saying he found a body on his way to work at the Yankton Sioux tribal offices in Wagner. He told authorities, "I saw a car there earlier, and a guy was looking in the ditch. I saw him looking, and I pulled over and saw something in the water. I stopped and looked over and saw what looked to be a body." After seeing the body, he drove the half-mile to the Yankton Sioux Alcohol Treatment Program office nearby and called authorities. He told them the body was clothed and floating in about four feet of water in the ditch between Highway 281 and the railroad tracks, on the south side of the lake.

Authorities arrived and recovered the body, and although it was badly decomposed, they were able to make a positive identification through a tattoo on the ankle. Her mother also identified her at the morgue. It was Ruby Ann Bruguier. She was found 75 feet from where the accident occurred three months earlier. When she was found, she was in the same clothing as the night of the accident, but her glasses and shoes were missing. They were never found.

After the discovery of Ruby's body, law enforcement and recovery teams decided to pump the ditch to see if Arnold might be there as well. They began that evening, and just before noon the next day, March 11th, they discovered Arnold's body about 15 feet away from where Ruby was found. He was not frozen to the ground, and unlike Ruby, his body showed very little decomposition. Quoting an interview in the television series Unsolved Mysteries, "his body was well kept, his color was fine." Investigators were not certain that the clothing he was found in was the clothing he was wearing the night of the accident, and adding to the mystery, a set of three keys was found in his pocket. One was a vehicle key, and the other two appeared to be house keys, none of which could be connected to Arnold. Authorities never discovered which vehicle or house the keys may have belonged to.

During the recovery of Arnold and Ruby's bodies from the ditch, a clump of hair was found on the edge of the road about 30 feet away from where Ruby's body was found. Forensic testing of the hair determined that it was Ruby's. Authorities would later state that there's no way that clump of hair could have remained on the edge of the road the entire three months Arnold and Ruby were missing.

The question of whether Arnold and Ruby could have been there all along is a hotly debated topic in the media and in the Lake Andes community. Then-Deputy Sheriff Bill Youngstrom stated he had several written affidavits from people who walked that ditch in search of Arnold and Ruby, and that those people were not connected to Arnold or Ruby in any way. He also stated that he personally walked those ditches and the area several times during the time that the couple was missing, and never found a trace of them.

Additionally, there are multiple pictures posted online, showing the searches for Arnold and Ruby, in which law enforcement searchers are walking on the ice-covered lake and ditch.

Youngstrom was skeptical about the possibility that the

bodies were there the whole time, saying, "The ditch area we're looking at is 100 yards by 25 yards wide with no access to any flowing water." A quote in a separate *Argus Leader* article about Youngstrom's suspicions states, "the following is what he does know and can release: The couple died of exposure but they did not die in the ditch."

Yet another online article from the *Argus Leader* says, "'Officials stated that the case was closed, that they did not suspect foul play in Arnold and Ruby's deaths, but that "they did not die there but were moved there."'

WITNESS SIGHTINGS:

After the discovery of the bodies, witnesses came forward, claiming to have seen a dark colored SUV-type vehicle, like a Ford Bronco, with two men inside it, parked close to the accident site, right before Ruby's body was found.

At one point a witness claimed to have seen Arnold, who she knew personally, with three other men on New Year's Eve. She'd walked up to their car, saw Arnold in the backseat with two young men, and asked if they were coming to the party. Arnold didn't speak, but the others declined and drove off. She informed authorities, who questioned them all. She agreed to take a lie detector test, which she passed. The two others who were in the backseat of the car with Arnold were questioned extensively, and they told officials that they were home all night. They also underwent a polygraph which detected deception, according to Deputy Sheriff Bill Youngstrom.

Five others also came forward stating that they'd seen Arnold and Ruby. Another witness claimed to have seen Ruby on January 20th in Wagner, 17 miles away.

After the bodies were discovered, States Attorney Tim

Whalen stated in an interview, "We have an individual who saw Ruby and Arnold get in a car after the accident, and the car headed east."

(It's not clear whether these sightings of Arnold and Ruby were reported to authorities before or after Arnold and Ruby's bodies were found.)

AUTOPSY REPORTS:

After they were found, Ruby and Arnold's remains were immediately sent to pathologist Dr. Brad Randall in Sioux Falls, SD. He determined that Arnold and Ruby both died of exposure, and that neither sustained any injuries from the accident. Also found in an article published by *Argus Leader*, "Randall said the autopsies don't rule out the chance that the couple died elsewhere and their bodies were later placed in the ditch. 'I'm not saying they did or didn't (die elsewhere). I don't have any evidence to suggest that they did' he said. 'Anything is possible.'" The article goes on to state, "Autopsy results do show the two most likely died about Dec. 12th. 'They were consistent with having died on the day of the accident,' he said. 'When you're that far back, you're dealing with weeks as an area of error.'"

Yet other online reports state that no time of death could be determined, and that medical examiners could not explain why Ruby's body was much more decomposed than Arnold's.

Though neither law enforcement nor medical examiners would say that foul play was suspected, then-Charles Mix County States Attorney Tim Whalen also said in an interview that the two "mostly likely didn't die where their bodies were found."

A second autopsy was done in Albuquerque, NM, using

photographs, reports, and other facts, (but not the bodies), which, according to two different articles, "revealed additional evidence to investigate" and "found different results." No information can be found on those results.

The determination of "exposure" baffles the family. Karen Tuttle, Arnold's aunt, stated in an interview, "I don't believe the bodies were there because if they weren't hurt, they wouldn't lay down and die." Family members also expressed their frustration with the way the case was handled, such as the fact that no photos exist of the accident scene. Deputy Youngstrom claimed he did take photos, but something went wrong and the negatives came out blank. The family also stated that if it had been a white couple, the case would have seen more priority, such as being placed on a nationwide computer search right after Arnold and Ruby went missing.

Online sleuths tend to attribute the mystery of Arnold and Ruby's deaths to simple exposure and possible negligence in the searches and subsequent investigation. But many, including Arnold and Ruby's families, the town of Lake Andes, and especially those in the Native American community, feel there are too many unanswered questions to reach that conclusion with any sense of satisfaction or peace.

For your consideration:
~ How can a determination be made, stating that they likely died on or about December 12th, when the bodies are in vastly different stages of decomposition? Especially after 3 months time?
~ If they both died that day, in that ditch, in the same body of water, (she was found "floating in four feet of

water," according to Mr. Song Hawk's statement, not frozen to the ground) Arnold was found not far away under water, wouldn't they be in (more) similar states of decomposition?

~ Multiple reports and online articles state that Arnold's body was not frozen to the ground (under the water). (Was this point made intentionally, like a tipoff?) Why would his body not float to the surface like Ruby's had? If he died on the same day as Ruby, wouldn't his body have been *at least* advanced enough in decomposition to float?

~ It's understandable if Ruby's body had been more exposed that it would be more advanced in decay than Arnold's, but according to multiple reports and a once-published photo of Arnold, he looked as if he had died merely days or even hours before he was discovered, in almost pristine condition. How can this be explained?

~ Is the discovery of the tuft of Ruby's hair significant? Granted, an animal could have dragged it off, but if she was, indeed, floating in four feet of water, as Mr. Song Hawk stated, how is this possible? Was Ruby floating in four feet of water or not?

~ What "additional evidence to investigate" or "different results" did the second autopsy reveal? Why is there no mention of those results to the public?

~ As Karen Tuttle stated, "If they weren't hurt, they would not lay down and die." If there were no injuries to speak of, how did they die, exactly? If exposure is to be the official cause of death, and we are to believe they were in the ditch the whole time, how were they not discovered that night? How, even if they were intoxicated, would they not have been able to reach town? If they had the presence of mind to escape the car, wouldn't they also have the mental capacity to seek shelter in town, less than a mile away?

~ If, in fact, the ditch wasn't frozen over, and they fell into the (not deep) water, couldn't they have simply crawled out? If they had been rendered unconscious, (which would also have shown up in the autopsy reports as a concussion) and succumbed to the cold water that night, in that ditch, wouldn't they have drowned? Was there water in their lungs? If so, wouldn't cause of death be listed as drowning?

~ And, if the ditch were not frozen over (which multiple media sources and family have confirmed, that it was frozen over) and it was filled with standing water or partially frozen water, wouldn't the assumption be that the couple *could be* in the water? And wouldn't it have been dredged or pumped in an effort to find them that very day?

~ If they were in the ditch the whole time, and the ditch had no access to flowing water in or out, as the Deputy stated, why were Ruby's shoes and glasses never found?

~ What can be made of the keys in Arnold's pockets? Was he wearing his own clothing when his body was found?

~ Did Tracy get knocked out in the accident? How did they end up upside down simply by spinning out from a dead stop? Did Arnold and Ruby walk away, as she initially claimed, or was he gone when she came to, and then Ruby got out and disappeared?

~ Didn't Arnold and Ruby have coats on? Weathermen claimed the weather that day was freezing drizzle, but not subzero temps. Even with being intoxicated, how would they succumb to the cold so quickly? Especially if they weren't injured?

~ Given the repeated statements by law enforcement officials and States Attorney Whalen that they "did not die there, but were moved there," how can they *also* state that there was no foul play? Is that not a contradiction? How can it be both? Wouldn't that, in fact, be a *confirmation* that there was foul play? Or do people *commonly, innocently,* and *unintentionally* move bodies after they find them?

~ Why would *anyone* move their bodies, under *any* circumstances? And wouldn't moving them back to the accident scene seem more suspicious than just leaving them in the woods or somewhere else, since the accident scene had been so thoroughly searched?

~ AND, if they didn't die there, but were moved there, how can medical examiners claim they both died the same day? If authorities and medical examiners are going to adhere to their claims they decomposed at different rates because one was more submerged/protected by the water they were found in, wouldn't it also contradict their claims that they were moved there? How could they have decomposed at different rates if they'd died the same time *elsewhere,* and *not* in the water?

~ Who was the witness that saw the couple get into a car right after the accident? Was it the same person who found Tracy and rescued her? Wouldn't it stand to reason that someone witnessing Arnold and Ruby getting in a car right after the accident would likely also be the one who rescued Tracy?

~ How long was Tracy trapped in the car before she was rescued?

~ Is there a lot of traffic on this road at 6 a.m.?

~ There is no further information on the other person Mr. Song Hawk saw at the accident site the morning he found Ruby. Was that the dark colored vehicle with two men in it? Did they leave? Or did the other person Mr. Song Hawk saw stay and give a statement to authorities as well?

~ What happened to the photos taken at the accident

scene? How were they ruined? Was this a common issue or a one-off?

Even though this case is considered "closed" by authorities, if you know anything about the deaths of Arnold Archambeau and Ruby Bruguier, please contact
Charles Mix County Sheriff's Office at (605) 487-7625
Or the FBI at (605) 334-6881
Or submit an anonymous tip to tips.fbi.gov or call (800) 225-5324

(Ref: *Argus Leader*; Unsolved Mysteries; Danita Bruguier)

Ruby Ann was a very beautiful, caring, kind-hearted young lady. As we were growing up together as sisters, we got along so well. At times, we would have our ups and downs, but other than that, we took care of each other.

And me, being older than her, I always looked out for her. Then we got older, lived our teenage years together, and at the age of 18, Ruby got pregnant with her baby girl, Erika. And only got to live another 16 months with her baby girl. But I sure miss her every day.

Danita Bruguier

*Photo courtesy of Danita Bruguier

Robert Ghostbear
Unsolved Death

Mid March, 2012, 45-year-old Robert Ghostbear, from Kyle, SD, arrived in Rapid City, SD, to visit his mother in the hospital.

A week later, on March 21st, two people walking near the railroad tracks on East North Street discovered Robert's body. He'd been beaten to death. A later autopsy showed he had died of blunt force trauma to the head.

Rapid City Police and the Pennington County Sheriff's Office opened a joint homicide investigation into Robert's murder, and are offering $6000 reward for information leading to an arrest and conviction in his murder.

RCPD Captain James Johns stated in an interview, "We've aggressively pursued every lead in the murder of Robert Ghostbear, but we don't have the information to make an arrest. Someone knows exactly what happened that day, and we're asking them to do the right thing and come forward."

Authorities are desperately trying to trace Robert Ghostbear's movements throughout his last day to see if anyone remembers seeing him, or seeing him with anyone.

For your consideration:

~ What possible motive would anyone have to harm Robert?

~ Are there witnesses who can tell authorities when he was last seen, and if so, why is no one coming forward?

If you know anything about the death of Robert Ghostbear, please contact

Rapid City Police Department at (605) 394-4134

Or Pennington County Sheriff's Office at (605) 394-6113

Or submit an anonymous tip by texting RCPD and the info to 847411

Or submit an anonymous tip online at www.rapidcitypolice.org

*Qualifying tips submitted anonymously are still eligible for rewards.

(Ref: *Rapid City Journal*; temp.rcgov.org)

Robert was a good man. Growing up, he and his brothers loved running and were known for it. They would run to school, several miles each day. He was particularly close to his older sister, Gladys, who helped raise him and his siblings until her death in high school.

Robert's brother, Myron, cried talking about Robert and his death. He said he missed his brother terribly, and whoever killed him wouldn't have a happy life.

Robert was an artist, and did magnificent beadwork. He and his brothers spoke Lakota and knew traditional songs. He did odd jobs to make money, working as a ranch hand, breaking horses, and chopping wood. He was always so helpful at wakes and funerals, and pitching in wherever help was needed. He was respectful, kind, and well liked. He is sorely missed.

Marilyn A. Charging Crow, sister-in-law

Serenity June Dennard
Missing Person

Serenity Dennard, 9 years old, was residing at the Black Hills Children's Home in Rockerville, SD, where she was receiving therapy for behavior issues. The Black Hills Children's Home treats children dealing with trauma, abuse, and mental and behavioral health issues.

Serenity began her stay at the Children's Home in July of 2018. Most stays are about 14 months long. She'd been in therapy for behavioral issues stemming from bouncing in and out of several foster homes after being removed from her biological parents. Serenity had been placed under special "arms-length-only" monitoring the week before when she attempted to run away. This monitoring was dropped a day or two before February 3, 2019. Serenity had a history of running, but usually stayed close by, and not for very long. She suffered from mood swings and reactive attachment disorder (RAD) from being shuffled from home to home.

On February 3, 2019, about 10:45 a.m., a woman dropping off a relative at the home noticed a young girl walking away from the building, and she and her granddaughter watch as Serenity stumbled across a cattle guard near Rockerville Road. The woman, suspecting Serenity was a runaway, reversed the car to the building and notified the staff inside.

The granddaughter remained in the car and watched Serenity as she went north on Rockerville Road until the granddaughter lost sight of her due to trees and topography, at about 11:20 a.m. Within three to four minutes of losing sight of Serenity the grandmother and granddaughter drove out the entrance and in the direction of where they last saw

Serenity, but did not see Serenity or any other vehicles.

According to multiple news reports, several other students were in the gym at the children's home with two staff members. When one child ran away within the building, apparently preplanned by Serenity and this child, one staff member ran after her, leaving one staff member in charge of the other students in the gym. That's when Serenity ran from the building. The staff member alerted the other staff, but chose to stay with the other children and not follow Serenity. Unfortunately, more valuable time was lost when staff realized that they were not all on the same radio channel when the alert went out.

After Serenity was reported missing, staff notified a supervisor at home, who advised them to continue searching for 15 minutes before contacting authorities. When the supervisor arrived at the facility 80 minutes later, authorities had still not been contacted. They then notified authorities.

Authorities received the call about Serenity at 12:26 p.m. and were at the facility by 12:45 p.m. Additional help, Pennington County Search and Rescue, arrived around 1:28 p.m.

Multiple, exhaustive searches were conducted in the search for Serenity, with more than 1500 people in over 200 separate searches over 6,000 miles of forest. All possible search techniques are employed in the search, including aircraft and thermal devices. Cadaver dogs picked up on a scent near a creek, but it was unknown if it was Serenity's scent, nor did it produce evidence of Serenity.

Law enforcement and other agencies, 66 total, followed hundreds of leads, and conducted hundreds of door-to-door searches and interviews, with no positive results.

Amid rumors that Serenity may have preplanned this with someone she'd had contact with prior to running away, investigators searched for all possible connections she may have made with someone by phone or computer. They found no evidence to indicate these rumors were true.

The weather was chilly the day Serenity left the home wearing only a long-sleeved shirt, jeans and snow boots, turning bad that night. Temps dipped below freezing, and it snowed, which stayed for several weeks. It's unlikely Serenity could have survived for more than a few hours in those conditions, Pennington County Sheriff Kevin Thom stated.

Serenity's adoptive parents, Chad Dennard and his wife, KaSandra, and Serenity's adoptive mother, Darcie Gentry (Chad's ex-wife), were all questioned and dismissed as suspects in Serenity's disappearance.

The two staff members in charge of Serenity that day have been fired. The Black Hills Children's Home has since made improvements to their security measures, including improved policies regarding contacting 911, installing a new phone system, and employing a designated supervisor on campus at all times. Security cameras are to be installed in both the Black Hills Children's Home and the Children's Home in Sioux Falls.

Serenity was 4'7" tall and weighed 96 pounds at her disappearance and has dark blonde hair and blue eyes. She was born on May 12, 2009. She was last seen wearing a gray, long-sleeved shirt with flowers, a purple tank top, dark blue stone-washed jeans, and black snow boots.

For your consideration:
~ Who was the friend who helped coordinate Serenity's

escape? Is there a reason Serenity felt it necessary to run away? What don't we know about this plan?

~ Why was the "arms-length-only" policy dropped right before she ran away?

~ No cars were seen in the area, either coming or going, being a remote area with only local traffic. How could Serenity have disappeared so fast from her last sighting? How can a 9-year-old hide so well with so many people searching for her?

~ Was she dragged away by an animal?

If you know anything about the disappearance of Serenity Dennard, please contact
   Pennington County Sheriff's Office at (605) 394-6113
   Or to submit an anonymous tip, text RCPD and your tip to 847411.

(Ref: Disappeared; *Rapid City Journal; KELOLAND News; Argus Leader; SD News Watch; KOTA TV)*

Serenity June came into our lives in the winter of 2014. I fell in love with her at first site! Her smile completely lit up the entire room, and just being near her, I felt like she had been my daughter from birth. She proudly gave me a tour of her current home, bedroom, and got out all of her toys for us to play with. I had tears in my eyes as I reluctantly left after our first meeting, and longed to hold my daughter again. The following days seemed forever long, as I waited for the foster-adoption process to keep moving.

Finally, Serenity got to come to our house for her first visit! I had decorated her bedroom and our home with pictures I took of us the first day we met her. She loved her bedroom colors and decorations, the new toys we had ready for her, and meeting her new brothers! The day was such a success, and we were even more eager to bring her home forever. The following days seemed to pass slowly, but the day did finally arrive where my daughter came home to stay!

Every day has been a blessing with Serenity. Yes, we have had our trials in the past, but we have also far-made up for those with moments of love and adoration. Serenity has such a bubbly personality, that even on her darkest days, she seems to spring back smiling and loving. Her voice is very unique, and a sound that I grew to love immediately. I would recognize it in crowds of people! She loves to sing, and knows every word of many songs - especially her and I's favorite movie, "Frozen." Her room is decorated in pinks and purples, "Frozen" blankets, and a beautiful hand-made blanket from a dear friend, who is eagerly waiting to meet her for the first time! Her stuffed animals and dolls are patiently waiting to be loved again.

Not a day goes by where I don't think of my daughter, and wonder what she is doing and who she is with, and hoping and praying that she is being loved until I have her back in my arms. She is my true "mini-me", and she has so much to give this world! The thought that keeps me going is believing that God will reunite us, which will be in His time. We will forever be waiting for our princess to return to us. We love you forever, Serenity June!

Love mom and Brian

*Photo courtesy of Darcie Gentry

Two Deaths

"Every man has two deaths, when he is buried in the ground and the last time someone says his name. In some ways men can be immortal."   ~ *Earnest Hemingway*

Say their names. Let all of these men, women, and children be immortal, or at least not forgotten.

Don't let them die again.

Everett and Louella Owens Unsolved Deaths

On Sunday, January 11, 1970, when Mrs. Louella Owens didn't show up at an Eastern Star practice, members of this organization became concerned. She'd been recently installed as a Worthy Matron (presiding president of the organization), and it was not like Louella to be late.

Upon reaching the rural Gettysburg residence of Louella Owens and her husband, Everett, Louella's friends found the home burning. Firemen were called at 3 p.m. and upon containing the blaze, they discovered the bodies of Everett, 47, and Louella, 49, dead in the kitchen. An autopsy showed they'd been shot with a high-powered rifle.

Fire department officials believed the fire had been intentionally set, finding evidence of fuel spread throughout the home before it was set afire. The house was almost completely destroyed. Investigators believed the Owens' were killed after returning home from church around noon, and that the fire was set afterwards, and it smoldered until friends showed up around 3 p.m. Chief Deputy Fire Marshall Joe Brown would later testify that the fire was an act of arson, having found "pieces of newspapers and magazines strewn about the unburned part of the living room."

Later that month, the Owens' son, Monte, 16, was arrested and charged with the murder of his parents. He was not home at the time the bodies were found. He pleaded not guilty to the charges, and was released on a $25,000 bond.

Monte was popular, well liked in school, and active in band, All State Chorus, track, football, and basketball. He had an older brother Raymond who was a medical student at the University of South Dakota in Vermillion.

District County Judge Leland Berndt ordered Monte taken to the state hospital in Yankton for psychiatric examination, and that his name be withheld.

On December 4, 1970, a jury of 10 men and two women found Monte Owens not guilty of the double murder of his parents. His brother Raymond attended the trial and left with Monte after he was released.

The case is still unsolved.

For your consideration:

~ Is it possible that a stranger entered the Owens' home while they were away, and ambushed them when they arrived home from church?

~ What possible motive would Monte have to harm his parents?

~ Were the Owens' victims of robbery?

~ Articles published about this murder don't mention the gun as evidence. Was a gun ever found? Did the Owens' own a gun like the one used to kill them?

~ Why would someone burn the house after shooting the Owens? Was there evidence they were trying to destroy?

~ Is there more to the story of the Owens than newspapers reported? What other evidence was there?

If you know anything about the murder of Everett and Louella Owens, please contact the Potter County Sheriff's office at (605) 765-9405.

(Ref: *Potter County News, 1970*)

Andrew Jon "A.J." Lufkins
Missing Person

Andrew "A.J." Lufkins, for the first night in a long time, decided to go out with friends and enjoy himself on the night of Wednesday, April 7, 2010. They stopped at the American Legion in Sisseton about 9:00 p.m. to use the restroom. Shortly afterward, according to a family member, A.J., 23, got into a fight with three other men at this bar, and he was seriously injured.

A.J.'s family member states the following: The bartender told them to take the fight outside, where the beating continued. After a few minutes, a witness to this fight told them that A.J. needed to go to the hospital because his head was bleeding badly. At that point, a female friend of A.J.'s and one of her friends agreed to take him to the hospital, and they loaded him into their pickup.

A.J. never arrived at the hospital.

Details about where A.J. went after leaving the American Legion are muddy. Witness statements are inconsistent and no trace of A.J. has been found since. Security cameras outside the American Legion that night were not working. The City Municipal across the street had cameras, but they didn't catch the disturbance at the American Legion.

Andrew "A.J." Lufkins was last seen by multiple witnesses being carried from the American Legion in Sisseton, SD, unconscious. He is American Indian, a member of the Sisseton Wahpeton Oyate Indian Tribe. Andrew is 6'1" tall and 160 pounds. He has black hair and brown eyes and has a tattoo of his initials on the top of his wrist of his left hand.

At the time of his disappearance, he was wearing a dark blue or black hooded sweatshirt with a South Pole logo on the front, a dark-colored jersey with light blue accents over the sweatshirt, a white t-shirt under the sweatshirt, tan pants, or blue jeans, a blue bandana and blue and white K-Swiss sneakers.

In a related case, according to FBI, Minneapolis Division, "Michael Todd Never Misses A Shot, age 38, was indicted by a federal grand jury on April 4th, 2012, for making a false statement. The indictment alleges that he made false statements to an FBI agent regarding the disappearance of Andrew Jon (A.J.) Lufkins, who was last seen in Sisseton in April 2010. Since that date, county, tribal, state, and federal law enforcement officials have been involved in a joint investigation to determine Lufkins' whereabouts and whether he was the victim of foul play. The investigation remains open, and anyone with information should contact law enforcement.

Never Misses A Shot appeared before U.S. Magistrate Judge John E. Simko on April 10, 2012. The maximum penalty upon conviction is five years' imprisonment and a $250,000 fine. The charge is merely an accusation, and Never Misses A Shot is presumed innocent until and unless proven guilty.

The investigation is being conducted by the South Dakota Division of Criminal Investigation and the FBI. Assistant U.S. Attorney Dennis R. Holmes is prsecuting the case. Never Misses A Shot was remanded to the custody of the U.S. Marshals Service. A trial date has not yet been set." (Also stated: This content has been reproduced from its original source. – U.S. Attorney's Office, District of South Dakota)

For your consideration:
~ Who was responsible for getting A.J. to the hospital? What is their explanation for his not showing up at the hospital?

~ Who else was in the vehicle with the person who drove A.J. to the hospital? What was their statement about A.J.'s whereabouts?
~ The hospital has no record of A.J.'s arrival. If A.J. was unconscious and bleeding, why did they not take him to the hospital?
~ Who did A.J. fight in the bar? Who witnessed this fight?
~ Some witnesses claim that the people who took A.J. to the hospital returned to the bar later on that night. Did no one question them then? How far could they have gone?
~ Why would anyone want to keep A.J. away from medical help or even his family?

Andrew's family has expressed that they only want him home, and that no one need go to jail. A reward for any information that leads to A.J.'s physical location now stands at $25,000.

If you know anything about the whereabouts of Andrew Jon "A.J." Lufkins, please contact the South Dakota DCI Watertown office at (605) 773-3331

Or the Desoto County Sheriff's Department at (662) 429-1470

Or the FBI at tips.fbi.gov or call 1(800) 225-5324

Or submit an anonymous tip at Sisseton.com/tip.

*Qualifying tips submitted anonymously are still eligible for reward money.

(Ref: *Dakota News Now;* The Charley Project; The Doe Network; FBI – MPLS Division; Lufkins family)

A.J. always made everyone smile. He knew how to make everyone laugh and smile, especially when they were sad. He was a happy person, and spoke his mind. He let it be known what he thought.

My brother would always check on my grandmas and grandpas. He loved his grandpa, and always wanted to be with him. He was the only man in A.J.'s life.

He always took my kids from me when he knew I was stressed out and needed help. He would stay up at night with my son who was six months old.

He loved everybody he knew, and he did whatever he could to help anyone, even if it was his last dollar.

Ida Jack

*Photo courtesy of Ida Jack

Lawrence Steiger and Renae June Uithoven Unsolved Deaths

Around noon on Sunday, February 2, 1975, officers in Winner, SD, found 71-year-old Lawrence Steiger and 36-year-old Renae June Uithoven shot to death in his mobile home. Then-Tripp County Sheriff Darrell Meiners said the shooting happened around 2 a.m. Sunday morning.

The home, located in Pisha Trailer Court at 322 Harding Street in Winner belonged to Lawrence Steiger. Renae June Uithoven of Kennebec had been staying with him. The couple was found in the hallway, shot three times in the side. No information about the murder weapon was released.

On Monday, February 3, Francis "Sonny" Peck of Pierre had been arrested in Hughes County on two counts of murder. Peck worked on a ranch in the Harrold area, northeast of Pierre, SD. He was transferred to the Tripp County Jail in Winner and a $100,000 bond was set.

An online article called *Dakota Yesterday* states that Lawrence had operated a pool hall in Kennebec, had befriended Renae, and offered her a place to stay away from Peck with whom she had an abusive relationship. This article states that Peck had driven to Winner on the night of the murder, and asked someone at the Westside Café directions to Lawrence Steiger's home.

According to the aforementioned article, Tommy Drake Tobin took control of the case, and along with then-Attorney General Bill Janklow, decided to dismiss all charges. Peck was released from jail.

Sadly, there are very few details about this case.

For your consideration:
~ Was there no physical proof tying Peck to the murders?
~ Why was a weapon not mentioned in the articles? Was there a weapon found?
~ What about the witness stating Peck asked for directions? Is this too circumstantial?
~ Are there other suspects? Are law enforcement officials still pursuing this case?

If you know anything about the double murder, please contact

The Winner Police Department at (605) 842-3324 or
The Tripp County Sheriff's Office at (605) 842-3600.

(Ref: *The Winner Advocate; Dakota Yesterday - John J. Simpson*)

Larissa Lone Hill
Missing Person

On October 3, 2016, 21-year-old Larissa Lone Hill left her mother's house to go to the mall and later texted her cousin to say she was with two male friends. She was never seen again.

Larissa had lived on the Pine Ridge Reservation. Wanting to be closer to her little girl, who was in the custody of the little girl's father's family, she had moved the 100 miles to Rapid City to live with her older sister Carol.

On October 2nd, Larissa and Carol had an argument, and Carol had told her she needed to move out. Larissa then went to visit her mother, Lisa, who told her to go back to Carol's and make it right. Lisa suspected the argument could have been because of Larissa's struggles with drugs.

That same day, Larissa's boyfriend, Robert Mayes, and a girl named Virginia came by Lisa's house. Larissa told Lisa that she, her boyfriend, and Virginia were going to go to the Rushmore Mall and hang out. As Lisa watched them walk off toward the mall, she felt a foreboding sense that it might be the last time she ever saw her daughter again.

The next day, Larissa's cousin, Mariah, got a text from Larissa saying that she was with two guys, and she was going to a party.

A few days went by and Larissa's boyfriend became alarmed when he didn't hear from Larissa. He went to Larissa's brother, who then filed a missing persons report with the police department in Rapid City.

When the police questioned Larissa's boyfriend, he stated that two guys who Larissa had described as her cousins had picked her up at his home. Larissa's family told police that these men were not related to Larissa.

When the police found the two young men, one denied seeing Larissa at all, and the other stated that he had picked Larissa up and dropped her off at a party. He said he left and hadn't seen her since.

Police have stated they have reason to believe Larissa is no longer alive and buried somewhere within 100 miles of Rapid City.

Larissa was a loving mother to her 2-year-old daughter, often hitchhiking or walking miles to spend time with her. Though Larissa struggled off and on with drugs, she was a hard worker and a loving, caring person who liked to help out and enjoyed children.

Larissa is Native American, a member of Lakota Indian Tribe, with brown hair and brown eyes. She is 5'3" and weighs about 130 pounds. Her nickname is Rissa or may use the name Lisa. She has a tattoo of a paw print on her hand, and also has tattoos of the names, "Mom," "Lisa," and "Luda" elsewhere on her body.

For your consideration:

~ Who are the people Larissa partied with after the young men dropped her off?

~ Why did the one young man deny even seeing her, when the boyfriend clearly stated that there were two men that picked her up? Are these two young men suspects?

~ Did Larissa accidentally overdose and the partygoers panicked and hid her body?

~ Why would Larissa tell her boyfriend that the two young men were her cousins when she was not related to them in any way? Was she desperate to leave and needed to give her boyfriend the impression that she was related to them so he wouldn't be jealous?

~ What makes police believe she's buried within 100 miles of Rapid City?

~ Did Larissa simply walk away from her life?

~ In one online article, Larissa's mother stated that she didn't know where Larissa got her spending money. Was she knowingly or unknowingly involved with something or someone that got her killed?

Rapid City Police are offering a $5,000 reward for information on the location of Larissa's body, so her family can bring her home.

If you know anything about Larissa Lone Hill's disappearance, please contact

Rapid City Police Department at (605) 394-4134

Or Tribal Police at (605) 867-5111

Or to submit anonymously, text the RCPD at 847411

Photo courtesy of Lisa Lone Hill

(Ref: *Rapid City Journal; KELOLAND News*; The Charley Project; Lisa Lone Hill)

When Larissa went missing, her 4-year-old little girl said, "Mama went for a long walk."

We miss Larissa's beautiful smile. She was so caring and helpful. I loved to cook, so Larissa wanted to feed everyone she saw who was hungry.

When she came to Rapid City, she only wanted to raise her daughter. She loved to help out, never complaining. She always let us know where she was. It's not like her to be gone without telling us where she would be. It will be six years, now, that she's gone. We can't believe it.

When Larissa was in school, she liked to write poetry and wanted to be an artist.

She wrote a beautiful letter to me, which I will always cherish.

"I am thankful for my mother because she's always there for me, no matter what. She loves me as much as I love her, and she makes me happier than anything in the world. I don't know what I'd do without her.

I am thankful for her because she's a hard-working mother.

She's always on her feet, and using her hands for the work she does. My mom goes to work for us every day so she can pay the bills and buy us new things. She works hard all the time, and when she comes home, she's still cleaning. She always makes sure the dishes are done before and after we eat. She always cooks for us; that's why we're never hungry

I love my mom because she takes good care of us. She cooks the best food ever. My mom has strong working hands because she makes bread all the time, and it's the best bread ever. I say she has strong hands because when she makes a lot of bread, she has to roll it out and kneed it and that looks like a lot of work.

My mom is the Best Mom in the whole world. I love her with all my heart, like she loves us, too. I am very thankful for my mom because without her, I am no longer me. I can't live without her ~ Larissa"

Lisa Lone Hill

*Photo courtesy of Lisa Lone Hill

Monica Lou Bercier Wickre Unsolved Death

In 1993, Monica Bercier Wickre, also known as "Mona," was a married mother of three, and living in Aberdeen, SD. Her two older children lived with their father, Monica's first husband, in North Dakota, but she saw them often.

On April 7th, Monica Wickre got a ride from her husband to a local club where she and her friends were meeting to have a couple drinks after work at Indian Health Service. Her daughter stated in a Dateline interview that Monica liked to socialize and her husband did not, but that this arrangement seemed to work for them.

Monica was last seen at a now-closed bar called The Body Shop. As Monica hadn't driven there, she got a ride from a couple she knew and another man whom she didn't know. Reports claim that the couple dropped the man off at his car, and Monica opted to go with him. That was the last time Monica was seen alive.

Monica was close with her nine siblings who lived in Aberdeen and in ND. Her parents, John and Metha Bercier, lived on the Turtle Mountain Band of Chippewa reservation where Monica was born and raised. When none of them had seen or heard from her in two weeks, they became alarmed and contacted Monica's husband and the Aberdeen Police Department. A missing persons report was filed on April 26th, almost three weeks after she was last seen.

Multiple searches ensued throughout Aberdeen and surrounding areas, but no trace of Monica was found.

In June, canoeists on the James River just outside of Aberdeen discovered a decomposed body in the river. Authorities identified the body as Monica's through dental records. Though a cause of death could not be found due to advanced decomposition, authorities suspected foul play and considered her death a homicide.

The case file continues to grow through law enforcement's investigation into her death, and authorities have suspects in mind, but none of them have been named or charged. Authorities have stated that they do not have enough evidence to pursue prosecution.

For your consideration:
~ Though authorities say there was a good reason for the time gap that she was not reported missing, why did it take so long for Monica's husband to report her missing?
~ Did the couple that gave Monica the ride know the man who was also along and with whom Monica left?
~ Was there any DNA evidence found on Monica's body? Is it still possible to pursue forensic evidence?
~ Authorities state that there are "suspects" – plural. Does that mean there are several who are being considered, or is there a possibility that more than one person is responsible for Monica's death?

There is a $10,000 reward for any information leading to the arrest and conviction of Monica's murder.

If you know anything about the murder of Monica Wickre, please contact
The Brown County Sheriff's Department at (605) 626-7100 (lead investigating)
Or The Aberdeen Police Department at (605) 626-7000
Or submit an anonymous tip to (605) 626-3500.
*Qualifying anonymous tips are still eligible for rewards.
(Ref: Dateline; *NBC News; Aberdeen News; Argus Leader*; Tonya Hertel)

Our mom is very loved and we miss her deeply. She truly had a smile that would light up the room. She was so much fun to be around—always dancing, singing, and making people laugh. She sang on TV, at talent contests, and at various local events throughout her life, winning the hearts of many.

Our mom had a big heart, gifting people, keeping in touch with her big family, helping when she could.

There's so much I could say, but mostly, she's still very loved and missed.

Tonya Hertel

*Photo courtesy of Tonya Hertel

Delema Lou "Babe" Sits Poor
Missing Person

Somewhere around February 1, 1974, 12-year-old Delema Lou "Babe" Sits Poor and a friend, also 12 years old, decided to walk the back roads from Oglala to Manderson on the Pine Ridge Reservation. According to multiple news articles, the temperature was sub-zero.

Oglala, SD, is southwest of Manderson, SD. The distance between Oglala and Manderson, as the crow flies, is 12.99 miles. By car, the main route following White Horse CK road goes south and back northeast and totals 26 miles, almost an hour's drive. With reports of the girls traveling the back roads, one can assume those back roads followed the shorter distance. But the terrain directly between Oglala and Manderson is quite hilly, with only winding dirt roads, if that, connecting the two.

Delema was a student at the Seventh Day Adventist School between Oglala and Pine Ridge.

Delema's friend, who is unnamed in any of the stories, turned back due to the cold, but Delema continued. Delema's friend, it is reported, suffered frostbite on her hands and feet.

Delema was never seen again.

Very little information exists about Delema's disappearance. One report claims that she was seen near the Red Cloud Indian School, southeast of Oglala. (This would contradict earlier claims that she took the back roads. This school is located on the main road to Manderson.)

Delema was born November 21, 1961. She was 5'5" and about 135 pounds at the time of her disappearance, and has brown hair and brown eyes. She was last seen wearing a white down jacket with brown stripes on each sleeve, brown bell-bottom pants, and sneakers.

For your consideration:
~ Who is the unnamed friend?
~ Why were the girls determined to travel so far on foot? Especially in such bitterly cold weather? What was so important that it meant risking their lives to walk the 26 miles? Were they running away?
~ No trace of Delema is ever found. Was Delema picked up by someone? If they were following a dirt road, who could possibly be out on that back road in February?
~ If Delema succumbed to the cold, wouldn't there be *some* trace of her found along the road they traveled? Perhaps she turned back as well and was picked up closer to Oglala?

If you know anything about the disappearance of Delema Lou "Babe" Sits Poor, please contact the Pine Ridge Police Department at (605) 867-8127
Or the Oglala Sioux Tribe Department of Public Safety at (605) 867-5141.

(Ref: Justice for Native People; The Charley Project; The Doe Network, Genevieve Ribitsch)

Delema was my cousin, but we were raised together, so she is my baby sister, the baby of the family. Then she was taken from us when she was 13 on February 4th, 1974. She was attending 7th Day Advent Christian School. She was a very quiet, happy person. She always had a smile on her face, a smile that nobody will ever forget. We love her a lot and never stop hoping that one day, we can have her back and our family can have a closure. She is being missed every day.
Genevieve Ribitsch

*Photo courtesy of Genevieve Ribitsch

If your loved one's case is not in this book and you would like to see it included in a possible second book, please contact me through my website at www.christinemagerwevik.com

Charles William "Mesu" Quiver Unsolved Death

On September 23, 2015, about 9 p.m., Rapid City police officers received a call about a man, Charles "Mesu" Quiver, who had just been assaulted at the corner of First and North Street. The officers arrived on the scene and found the victim lying on the street. The witnesses claimed two male suspects, one wielding a baseball bat, had run away on foot.

Charles, 49, was immediately transported to the hospital by ambulance where he died from his injuries.

Charles was described as "comfortable with his life" and Gypsy lifestyle. He had no known enemies and was a hard worker, traveling from place to place, job to job.

For your consideration:
~ Who would have a motive to harm Charles? With the string of several mysterious deaths about the time of Charles's murder and that most of them were Native American, could this have been racially motivated?
~ What, if any, evidence is there for law enforcement to pursue?
~ Witnesses saw two men leaving the scene but few details are published about them. What did they look like? Why not publish as many details as possible about these suspects?

If you know anything about the murder of Charles "Mesu" Quiver, please contact
The Rapid City Police Department at (605) 394-4134 or
Submit an anonymous tip by texting "RCPD" and the information to 847411.
(Ref: *Black Hills Pioneer*; Abbie (Bee) Quiver)

Charles William "Mesu" Quiver

My brother was born December 9th 1965 to Charles & Elaine Quick Bear Quiver at Pine Ridge SD.

I've decided that I must put on paper what I cannot say.

The phrase "Cool Customer" comes to mind because he lived life to the fullest in his own way. He was like a "Ghost"—here one day gone the next, gone to the next adventure. Sometimes I wondered where he was and when he would appear again.

Like a thief in the night he would appear, and say, "Sister I've been here, I've been there, I seen these relatives and those." We would laugh about his escapades.

No matter where I went, I looked for my Brother. It didn't matter where because he ended up in the most unexpected places. I would be somewhere and I would hear someone calling, "Sister!" I knew it would be him, as he is the only one to call me Sister.

He was a hard worker, no matter what, he pitched in and complained sometimes, but not very often, it was always,

"Well, let's get started and get it over with."

He learned how to do many things in his many, countless jobs. Said, "Sister, if someone shows me how to do something, I will remember. Because every time I meet someone or they hire me somewhere, I learn something new." Always keeping busy.

He spent the majority of his life in Rapid City. He was comfortable with his life. Sometimes I would ask him, "Brother, why don't you just stay with me?" His answer was always, "Because I don't want to stay in one place too long." For everyone who knew my brother you know this is the truth. I was comparing him to a Gypsy one day, and he said he should have been born during that time. I guess there is a lot to be said about living in the moment, because that's how my Bro lived. He accepted his lot in life, and had no regrets.

One of his many cousins called me and said, "He was always happy to see me no matter where I saw him, he always had something to tell me about. He will always be my friend." I thanked him and countless others for remembering my Brother.

I am thankful that he met many, many people on his many journeys and adventures. He shared that life is too short, and when he went he would be glad to see Mom again. But he would miss the people who he would leave behind. I wonder sometimes as I lay here at night waiting to lay him to rest if he knew he was nearing the end of this life's journey.

Somewhere, I read time will ease the pain. I wonder when that time will be, but again I know there is no escaping the pain. I'm only fooling myself if I think that time is the answer. My sister in law visited me and said we must keep our cherished memories for comfort and have faith.

Abbie (Bee) Quiver
*Photo courtesy of Abbie (Bee) Quiver

Bonnie Rose Jennesse
Unsolved Death

Bonnie Rose Jennesse, 33, was found about 11 a.m., September 28, 1984, crumpled at the bottom of a stairwell in a building in the 700 block of West 11th Street in Sioux Falls. Newspapers state that when she was found, she was confused and disoriented. She was taken to Sioux Valley Hospital and due to her severe injuries, she was placed on a ventilator. Four days later, on October 2, doctors determined that Bonnie had no brain activity and the decision was made to remove her from life support. She died the same day.

She was last seen by family the night before she was found in the stairwell. Although Bonnie was not known to be a drinker and was considered a "lightweight," she had agreed to go out with friends for drinks. She had been seen at the Arrow Bar near her home, left with someone, came back, and then left with someone else. That was the last time witnesses claimed to have seen her before she was found in the stairwell.

Bonnie Rose was the mother of seven children and worked as a nurse's assistant at Mom and Dad's Nursing Home. She had recently left an abusive marriage with her husband, Harvey, who was in jail at the time of her injuries and her death. Bonnie Rose was no stranger to violence, and she'd done everything she could to follow the proper channels to extricate herself from the ongoing abuse to herself and her children. She escaped to a shelter, filed for a protection order, and received a temporary protection order on May 10. The permanent order was granted on May

23. She filed for a divorce, and worked hard to provide for her children, never seeking financial aid. Her divorce was final on August 29.

After Bonnie was found in the stairwell, the officer on duty had no idea of her history with violence. He attributed her injuries and subsequent death to a fall, never questioning that she may have been attacked and left for dead. On Monday, Bonnie's lawyer, Karen Hattervig, discovered that Bonnie was in the hospital, and called the police station to ask how the investigation into Bonnie's injuries was proceeding. She learned there was no investigation, but her inquiry started an investigation into the possible assault on Bonnie Rose.

After Bonnie's death, an autopsy was performed by Dr. Brad Randall, and those results have not been shared with the public or family because the case is still considered "open." However, the certificate of death states that Bonnie's cause of death was listed as "accident," the date of injury was 9/28/84, and under the heading of "How Accident Occurred," are the words "fall down stairs."

In interviews with the *Argus Leader*, Sioux Falls Police Captain Don Skadsen said, "she died from a single blow to the back of her head, which appeared to have been sustained from within several hours from when she was found." He went on to say, "How the blow occurred, I don't know. I can't rule out that she was not struck, but her injury is more consistent with a fall." Blood and hair samples were collected in the stairwell where she was found and sent to the state crime lab, and though they were likely Bonnie's, there are no media reports online stating what the results revealed.

It's clear that Sioux Falls police feel that Bonnie's cause

of death was likely from a fall, but the case remains open because, according to a family member, tips surfaced from nine witnesses who refused to come forward with more information out of fear of retaliation. In an *Argus Leader* article, Sioux Falls police encouraged anyone who may have seen Bonnie on Thursday night or Friday morning to contact their department.

Bonnie Rose's case is still open.

For your consideration:
~ If SFPD are convinced this was simply an accident, why is the case still open? Might there be more evidence to support an attack on Bonnie Rose?
~ Was an analysis done to determine how Bonnie may have sustained the single wound to the back of her head, perhaps if she'd fallen backwards, where her head would have hit the steps, and how no other injuries to her head were found, etc?
~ Would a fatal fall down a set of stairs typically produce more than one injury?
~ If Sioux Falls police know of these nine witnesses, is the danger of retribution past, so they can possibly interview these witnesses again, and maybe pursue the suspects with whom Bonnie was last seen?

If you know anything about the death of Bonnie Rose Jennesse, please contact the
Sioux Falls Police Department at (605) 367-7212

(Ref: *The Argus Leader*; Janice Jennesse)

Bonnie Rose (Cane) Jennesse, enrolled Sicangu (Rosebud Sioux) Lakota, was born on January 20th 1951 in Gregory South Dakota to Eleanor (LeClaire) Cane and Thomas Cane. Bonnie Rose and her siblings grew up in the Milk's Camp Community on the Rosebud Reservation. She had one sister Clementine Cane and 5 brothers: Everett, Lars (Duane), Levi (Sonny), Reginald (Buddy) and Doug Cane.

Bonnie later met and married Harvey B. Jennesse through this marriage. It then became very apparent that her children were whom she lived for every day. She had 7 children, the eldest Shelly Rose, Edward Conrad, Almira Evangeline, Janice Tonia, Cleo Marie, Priscilla Lynn and Harvey Steve.

Bonnie, Harvey and their children started their life in Fort Thompson South Dakota, eventually relocating to Sioux Falls, South Dakota, where they resided until her abrupt death. Her 5th child, Cleo Marie had a degenerative disease that did not allow her to grow after about 1 ½ years old, Bonnie was not afraid to ask for help, so Cleo Marie was taken care of by local couple in Sioux Falls, that were able to give Cleo Marie 100% of their attention that unfortunately Bonnie couldn't due to having 6 other children. Bonnie still had 24/7 access to Cleo with visits that were allowed anytime, until Cleo's passing in July 1984.

It has always been said by both family and friends that Bonnie Rose was the most patient person with her children. At times she would be seen whether at home or in public, with her kids all crawling over her, as if she was jungle gym and she would sit still and continue to read her book. Bonnie Rose loved to read Harlequin romance novels that she could finish in a day or two. Therefore, she would go to this local bookstore that allowed people to exchange books versus having to pay for books to get more Harlequin novels.

Bonnie always made the best of her children's birthdays even during tough financial times. I, Janice, remember, she would purchase our birthday cakes at a local Hy-Vee store, bring it home and because it was my birthday, I would be the first to pick which part of the cake that I want. I remember my last birthday with her, we were all home, and I was so excited for my cake and ice cream. She went into the kitchen to see what our dad was doing, and he was trying to help her as best he could by scooping the ice cream onto plates and when he dug the scoop into the ice cream, the scoop broke and I remember us all laughing so hard at this moment and then she just picked up another big spoon to continue scooping. I don't ever remember her panicking over any part of birthday parties.

It goes without saying that Bonnie Rose was a very strong indigenous woman in a big city that despite of all her struggles she had to endure. Bonnie work full time as a nurse's aide at Mom & Dad's nursing home, which after her death, they added on a new addition to the nursing home, and it was named in her honor. She definitely had a lot of co-workers that cared deeply about her. One co-worker said she would take time for others in need, even if it was just providing someone with a ride home, after working the night shift. Another co-worker stated Bonnie was also very loved by the residents, as well as her co-workers.

Bonnie was beautiful, kind, hard working and always showed up for work. Bonnie was always immaculately dressed and had her hair in a braid or ponytail. The job at the nursing home was physically challenging and emotionally draining but she never complained or had a bad word to say about anyone or anything. When Bonnie would come pick up her paycheck, she would have all her little ones with her. They were so cute and so shy. They would hide behind her, and she was so proud of her kids. To prove Bonnie's hard work and dedication, she not only worked at the nursing home, but she was also a local housekeeper at a hotel/motel. Bonnie did everything she could to support and take care of her children to the best of her ability.

Bonnie Rose was also enrolled at a local community college (possibly Sioux Empire College) out of Hawarden Iowa that has since shut down in 1985, taking classes to become a nurse, having to drive 55 miles south of Sioux Falls, to attend her classes and sometimes having to take her children with her. One of my sister's remembers going with her and remembering an old building that looks like a gymnasium and just another building (that is what she remembers about the small college).

This being said about a wonderful mother, sister, aunt, cousin, niece, her family cannot make sense of why Bonnie was taken so abruptly with there being 9 witnesses afraid to come forward to law enforcement, as of the late 1990's. Her death is ruled accidental, on the death certificate, it states "head trauma" but no more information, due to a fall or blunt force trauma or any reason for the head trauma.

Bonnie's case is still open due to witnesses that were afraid to come forward at the time, to give her Justice, that is needed and deserved for her family to get closure.

My mother and father were divorced as of May 1984, and he was not ruled a suspect in her death due to his incarceration at the time of her death.

I hope this tribute helps people get a feel for what kind of woman she was. If anyone reading this has any information, even after 38 years, please come forward and currently, your information can remain anonymous to law enforcement in Sioux Falls, South Dakota and if you don't feel comfortable contacting law enforcement, then contact "Missing and Murdered Indigenous Women USA," Facebook page. They have also sworn on anonymity of any information regarding Bonnie Rose Jennesse.

Janice Jennesse

*Photo courtesy of Janice Jennesse

Michael Crawford
Unsolved Death

On November 10, 2015, at about 11 p.m., a neighbor in an apartment building at 24 Quincy Street, Rapid City, SD, heard someone banging on windows, trying to gain entrance to some of the other 4 apartments in the building. Shortly thereafter, though she did not hear a gunshot, she saw police at the scene, and found out that Michael Crawford, another tenant in the apartment building had died from a gunshot wound to the neck.

He was found behind his apartment building in the alley.

Though Michael lived alone, he was a best friend and constant companion of his ex-wife, Sabrina. At the time of his death, he worked for Environmental Services in Rapid City as a janitor.

A short time before the shooting, witnesses claim that Michael had been banging on the windows. According to Michael's ex-wife, someone in an upper apartment saw Michael and another person in the alley, and witnessed that person shooting Michael. The witness didn't get a clear view of the shooter.

When police arrived, they found Michael, and called for an ambulance. Michael passed shortly after arriving at the hospital.

For your consideration:
~ Was the shooting a result of Michael's erratic behavior?
~ Did Michael know his assailant?
~ With only a few possessions of any value, what

possible motive would anyone have to murder Michael?

If you know anything about the murder of Michael Crawford, please contact the

Rapid City Police Department at (605) 394-4134

Or submit an anonymous tip by texting RCPD and your info to 847411

(Ref: *Rapid City Journal;* Sabrina Crawford)

I'm Sabrina Crawford, Mike's last wife. I miss my best friend so much. We worked together always. I never needed a break from him. We were always together. We had the same upbringing. His father was raised in Quapaw, OK. My father was raised in Springfield, MO. Mike and I grew up five miles apart in Vancouver, WA. We really didn't know each other, but our families had the same friends. My brother went to school with Mike. They were 12 years older than me.

When I was 26, Mike and I met. I have never, ever met anybody who I got along with so well. We were so connected in so many ways; he was truly my best friend. I'm lost without him. Still to this day, I have not been in a relationship. No one compares.

We divorced in 2009, and I got married to another man, trying to move on with my life. Big mistake. That ended in divorce but I kept Mike's name.

Mike and I were always together, but lived a mile apart in South Dakota. We kept separate places for times that he would drink. He would go home and would come over to my place when he sobered up.

With Mike, we didn't have money to have an enjoyable day. He made life fun. Holidays have not been the same. There's a void in them without Mike. Mike would always greet me with a loud, joyful, "Hey, Baby!" Us girls miss him so much. Me and Marya live alone in Oklahoma now, trying to make a new life. But nothing fills the void. Mike would have been so proud of his four children. They all are good people. He is loved and missed by us. Mike always worked. He was a good provider, loved his children.

I guess you could say the pain is like a twin losing the other twin. He had such a loving side about him that most people didn't see. I was his Bree; he was always very happy to see me. We were always there for each other, even in an argument. We would help each other if the other really needed it. I miss my Michael.

Sabrina Crawford

*Photo courtesy of Sabrina Crawford

Carl Bordeaux
Unsolved Death

On a Friday night, on January 30, 2009, about 10 p.m., authorities found the body of Carl Bordeaux in his apartment at 1721 N. Maple Avenue in Rapid City, SD.

Bordeaux, 40, had been found with his throat cut and a phone cord wrapped around his neck. Rapid City Police Department Detective Steve Neavill stated in an interview with *KNBN NewsCenter1* that it was "one of the most egregious things he's ever seen" in his 24 years with the RCPD.

In that same interview, authorities stated that through physical evidence and multiple interviews they came up with several leads, but nothing that could lead to an arrest.

Police stated that Bordeaux lived alone, and neighbors said he kept to himself, but authorities believe the murder was committed by someone he knew and was not likely a random act. In the *NewsCenter1* interview, Neavill said, "It was done by someone who I believe was very close to Mr. Bordeaux." He also stated that he believed that a crime like this would be hard to keep to oneself, that something this traumatic might make someone want to tell another.

For your consideration:

~ Why do police believe the murder was committed by someone close to Mr. Bordeaux? Do they have specific evidence that might lead to a killer, given the right tip?

~ What possible motive would someone have to kill a

man who kept to himself? Was it robbery? Was it personal?

A $6,000 reward is being offered for information leading to an arrest and conviction in this case.

If you know anything about the death of Carl Bordeaux, please contact the
Rapid City Police Department at (605) 394-4134
Or submit an anonymous tip by texting RCPD and your tip to 847411

*Qualifying anonymous tips are still eligible for rewards.

(Ref: *KNBN NewsCenter1; Rapid City Journal*)

Victoria "Vicki" Eagleman Unsolved Death

It was summer of 2006 on the Lower Brule Indian Reservation, and Vicki Eagleman, 33, and her five children had just moved in temporarily with her mother, June Left Hand, and her stepfather, Richard, to get back on her feet. Throughout her short life, Vicki had been a longtime victim of domestic violence.

Victoria was looking for a new job, working temporary jobs and enjoying her time at home with her children in the meantime.

On July 28, 2006, between 11 a.m. and noon, Victoria had an errand to run and told her mother she'd keep in touch and let her know where she'd be. June watched Vicki disappear around the corner, not knowing that was the last time she'd see her daughter alive again. That afternoon, Jerilyn, Vicki's sister, who was also staying with June and Richard, said she and the kids were going swimming. At some point in the afternoon, Jeri picked up Vicki and her boyfriend, Bernard "Sonny" LaRoche, his sister, and her boyfriend. Details about what happened after they all got together and when they all parted are vague.

The next morning as he was getting ready for work, Vicki's stepfather noticed that Sonny, who was staying with them as well, was at home in bed but Vicki was not. He told June. Sonny told June and her husband that the last time he'd seen Vicki was the night before.

After a few hours, June became concerned when Vicki didn't arrive home and started calling friends and family, anyone she knew, asking if they'd seen Vicki. No one had.

When June couldn't find Vicki for several hours, she told her husband, who was on the Lower Brule police force, to inform his fellow officers and see if they could help find her. She states that law enforcement told her that Vicki was an adult and didn't need to account for her whereabouts, and that she was probably off partying. But June knew that Vicki would have checked in, as she usually did, calling and giving her mother a phone number where she could be reached if she wasn't going to be home for a while.

Between the time Vicki went missing and law enforcement got involved, June started receiving phone calls and messages from well-meaning friends and acquaintances, telling her "horrible stories," she says, about who killed Vicki and how. June stated that she had trouble sleeping afterward.

Weeks passed, and finally, BIA and the FBI start investigating, but no trace of Vicki was found.

Then, on August 22, the community organized a search. Trucks, ATVs, horses, walkers, over a hundred people joined in the search for Victoria in the small, tight-knit Lower Brule area. They searched everywhere in town and near the Missouri River but didn't find her.

On the second day of the search, August 23, Vicki's son, the eldest at age 12, ran home, sweaty and breathless, and told June, "Grandma, they found my mom!" He didn't know the awful truth. June Left Hand states that this date is incorrect, even though the newspapers and officials state it was August 23. June states that Victoria was found on August 28, a date she'll never forget.

Richard, who had helped in the search, was on the scene

when searchers discovered Victoria's body in a culvert along Medicine Creek, just off the Native American Scenic Byway in Lower Brule. She was naked, beaten to death, and had been stuffed into a culvert. After a recent heavy rain, her small body had washed out of the culvert, and according to one source, "her arms were stretched out, her hair flowing in an almost angelic pose."

Vicki's stepfather was in shock and had to be led away from the scene. As the only father Vicki and her siblings had ever known, he was devastated.

Autopsy results revealed that Vicki had died from blunt force trauma to the head with her face beaten in, and June was told it appeared she had been sexually assaulted.

The clothing Vicki had been wearing—a tan shirt with spaghetti straps, blue jean shorts, light blue scarf as a belt, and flip flop sandals—were never found. She'd also been wearing her mother's eyeglasses which were the same prescription as Vicki's, and a favorite fashion ring.

Police and FBI interviewed multiple people including Sonny, Vicki's boyfriend, but he is all but ruled out. Richard verified that Sonny was home about the time that June was told Vicki would have been killed, but the time of death and Sonny's exact whereabouts at that time cannot be proven. Vicki's ex-husband was also eliminated as a suspect, as he was stationed in Japan at the time.

Though authorities had several tips, and even suspects, no arrests have been made in Vicki's murder.

Months later after Vicki's funeral, her children found Vicki's eyeglasses that she had been wearing that day, smashed, and her ring, about a block from their home. The items were turned over to police.

Throughout the next several months and years, little progress has been made in her case.

In 2006, Vicki's case file including crime scene photos, was found in the former BIA police station and laying outside on the ground in Lower Brule along with another person's files. The person who found them returned it to the police department.

For your consideration:
~ There is no mention of forensic evidence in any online sources. Did authorities recover any DNA evidence from Vicki's body?
~ The investigator had told June that Vicki had likely been raped. Would that eliminate Sonny and likely point to another suspect?
~ Is there any significance to Vicki's glasses and ring being found only a block from her home?
~ Who had access to Vicki's case files? Why were they left behind after the police moved to a different location? Why weren't they kept in a secure location? Will this affect her case and the investigation if more evidence becomes available to authorities?

The FBI is offering a $15,000 reward for information leading to the arrest and conviction of Victoria Eagleman's killer.

If you know anything about the death of Victoria Eagleman, please contact
The FBI Pierre Resident Agency at (605) 224-1331 or
South Dakota State Radio at (605) 773-3536

Or submit an anonymous tip at tips.fbi.gov

*Qualifying anonymous tips are still eligible for rewards. (Ref: Justice For Native People; FBI; *KARE 11; Rapid City Journal*; Podchaser.com; June Left Hand)

Sat up till around 2 a.m., maybe later, thinking if you were here, you'd be either sitting, talking about how we could help one of the children. I wanted to cry, but held up, and thought it through. A lot has changed, as you can see. I can imagine the pain and love your feeling for your children. I'm doing my best, Vicki, some think I made some wrong decisions, but I did and will continue to do what is best, right and with prayer in all that I say and do for your children. Same for your nieces and nephews. I miss you, think of you daily, imagining you'd walk in that door one day.

Another Holiday and I'm sitting here thinking of you. This year has been a long and difficult one, but we made it through. I'm sure you can see, and hear everything that's been happening. Most of it not so good, in some ways, it's ok you aren't here, but then again you would have been that shoulder to help keep me upright. Past few months I have been really angry, with others, especially relatives.

I wished things were back to those many ago. Although not perfect, we all seem to be together, and all kept in contact one way or another. Now, everyone is hell bent on hurting each other for no damn good reason, well not to me. As you know I have learned as I have gotten older to control my tongue, which is hard as I have an answer and question to everything that is said, but I keep my mouth shut. In silence, my heart hurts, I cry inside, and days where I am so tired of all this bull, I lay down and cry myself to sleep.

I miss you so much, I know you know that I love you very much, but I'm sorry for not saying it as often as I should have. Each and every time a relative or friend has passed on, all the memories come flooding back, like it was yesterday they found you. They tell me time heals, but it doesn't. It's been so many years now. You are with Tara now, and I did make it to her funeral. She used to come visit me with Phil and all their kids. I'm going to miss her, too, especially her laughter, her smile, and attitude, like a breath of fresh air. Ask the spirits to come comfort Phil and his children. I know it's very hard for them right now.

As you already know I say my prayers and make my offerings like usual, which also helps me. Your children are doing okay, then not so okay, at times. I'm at a loss as to what to say or do to make things better for each of them. Also your nieces and nephews, they have their ups and downs. I don't like to see any of them hurting, or being hurt, so I talk to them, pray for them, and I'm still here.

Tell mother/grandma/great grandmother that I said hello,

as well as the rest of the grandmothers, grandfathers and relatives who are there with you.

It's been so many, many long years, each year it begins, maybe closer to my seeing you.

I am sad.
I love and miss you.
Mom

*Photo courtesy of June Left Hand

Acknowledgements

Thank you, first of all, to all the families who shared their time, loving tributes, photos, and hearts with me in our collective effort to seek justice for their loved ones.

Thank you to *KELOLAND News* for its extensive coverage of South Dakota's cold cases. KELOLAND Media Group was awarded the prestigious Edgar R. Murrow Award in 2021 for its excellence in digital coverage with its website KELOLAND.com.

Thank you to award-winning investigative reporter and 2022 SD Hall of Fame Inductee, Angela Kennecke for her contribution to this project, and for her fearless determination and dedication to seek the truth about these and other cold cases.

Thank you to Brenda Donelan, Samantha Lund Hillmer, Marilyn Kratz, Susan Miskimmins, Donna Neuman, Doreen Ronning, Loretta Sorensen, and Daniel Wevik for all your technical, design, literary, and emotional support.

Thank you to my husband, Doug, and my children, Valerie, Ashley, Kara, and Daniel for listening to me whine.

Finally, thank you to law enforcement officials throughout the state who shared whatever knowledge they could, and who continue to pursue answers and justice for these victims and their families.

About the Author

Christine Mager Wevik is the author of three other books. Her first, It's Only Hair is a humorous, self-help book about living and coping with hair loss and baldness. Vacant Eyes, her first novel, is an award-winning paranormal mystery. Borrowed Memories, second in the series, was awarded the Silver Falchion Best Supernatural Book of 2020, and Silver Falchion Best Book of the Year for 2020. Chris is the mother of four and grandmother of four, and lives in rural South Dakota with her husband Doug. Learn more about Christine and her work at https://christinemagerwevik.com.

www.ingramcontent.com/pod-product-compliance
Lightning Source LLC
LaVergne TN
LVHW021951060526
838201LV00049B/1661